XSLT Interview Questions, Answers and Explanations

Compiled By Terry Sanchez-Clark

XSLT Interview Questions, Answers and Explanations

ISBN 10: 1-933804-39-4
ISBN 13: 978-1-933804-39-2

Compiled By Terry Sanchez-Clark
Edited by Emilee Newman Bowles

Printed in the United States of America

Please visit our website at www.itcookbook.com

Table of Contents

Introduction

What is XSLT?

XSLT is Extensible Style Sheet Language Transformation (XSLT). It handles and formats the contents of Extensible Markup Language (XML) documents.

In recent years, there has been the mass usage of XML. And while XML allows and facilitates the structure of data in documents, XSLT enables you to work, manipulate and create the contents of XML documents. One example is the sorting of a particular database such as inventory of products, employee records, data files, and catalogues. XSLT allows you to get as detailed as possible in formatting and manipulating these database records.

You can work with the contents of XML documents by writing your own programs that interface to XML parser applications, but that involves writing your own code. With XSLT, on the other hand, you can perform the same kinds of tasks, and there's no programming required. Rather than write your own Java, Visual Basic, or C++ code to handle the contents of XML documents, you just use XSLT stylesheets to specify what you want to do, and an XSLT processor does the rest. That's what XSLT is all about, and it's becoming the next big thing in the XML world.

Functions and Uses

XSLT (a comparatively easy transformation language) and XPath (its companion specification for identifying parts of XML documents) make XML powerful and flexible. Using XSLT you can convert XML into display formats such as HTML, PDF, and Braille; make XML into application-specific formats such as typesetting languages; and automatically add numbering, cross-references, tables of contents, and generated text. You can even use XSLT to convert your XML documents into someone else's tag set.

Question 1: XML to XML Using XSLT

I would like transform my XML file to another XML file with a different format. I've managed to get the format the way I wanted it, but I'm only getting the first record of the original XML file duplicated in the output XML file. Below is an example of my XML data and style sheet.

```
<b>sample origional xml</b>

- <ABWTransaction Version="5.4"
xmlns:sql="urn:schemas-microsoft-com:xml-sql">
  <Interface>B1</Interface>
  <BatchId>YPO</BatchId>
- <Voucher>
  <VoucherType>94</VoucherType>
  <CompanyCode>W5</CompanyCode>
  <VoucherDate />
- <Transaction>
  <TransType>GL</TransType>
  <Transdate>2006-04-27T16:54:31.347</Transdate>
  <TaxCode>P2</TaxCode>
  <Number1>000100</Number1>
  <InvoiceNo>714208</InvoiceNo>
  <Dim7 />
  <Dim1 />
  <Description>SINGLE HOLE MINI PUNCH</Description>
  <Currency>GBP</Currency>
  <CurrAmount>00000050</CurrAmount>
  <Amount>00000050</Amount>
  <Account>0000</Account>
  <RecordID>1</RecordID>
  </Transaction>
- <Transaction>
  <TransType>GL</TransType>
  <Transdate>2006-04-27T16:54:31.347</Transdate>
  <TaxCode>P2</TaxCode>
  <Number1>000100</Number1>
  <InvoiceNo>722715</InvoiceNo>
  <Dim7 />
  <Dim1 />
  <Description>EXECUTIVE FOLDOVER CLIP
BOARD</Description>
  <Currency>GBP</Currency>
  <CurrAmount>00000098</CurrAmount>
  <Amount>00000098</Amount>
  <Account>0000</Account>
```

```
  <RecordID>2</RecordID>
  </Transaction>
- <Transaction>
  <TransType>GL</TransType>
  <Transdate>2006-04-27T16:54:31.347</Transdate>
  <TaxCode>P2</TaxCode>
  <Number1>000100</Number1>
  <InvoiceNo>763217</InvoiceNo>
  <Dim7 />
  <Dim1 />
  <Description>A4 CUT FLUSH FOLDERS ASST COL PK
25</Description>
  <Currency>GBP</Currency>
  <CurrAmount>00000095</CurrAmount>
  <Amount>00000095</Amount>
  <Account>0000</Account>
  <RecordID>3</RecordID>
  </Transaction>
- <Transaction>
  <TransType>GL</TransType>
  <Transdate>2006-04-27T16:54:31.347</Transdate>
  <TaxCode>P2</TaxCode>
  <Number1>000100</Number1>
  <InvoiceNo>313173</InvoiceNo>
  <Dim7 />
  <Dim1 />
  <Description>SCISSOR 15CM STAINLESS
STEEL</Description>
  <Currency>GBP</Currency>
  <CurrAmount>00000140</CurrAmount>
  <Amount>00000140</Amount>
  <Account>0000</Account>
  <RecordID>4</RecordID>
  </Transaction>
- <Transaction>
  <TransType>GL</TransType>
  <Transdate>2006-04-27T16:54:31.347</Transdate>
  <TaxCode>P2</TaxCode>
  <Number1>000100</Number1>
  <InvoiceNo>761702</InvoiceNo>
  <Dim7 />
  <Dim1 />
  <Description>A4 OVERSIZED PUNCHED POCKETS PK
100</Description>
  <Currency>GBP</Currency>
  <CurrAmount>00000470</CurrAmount>
  <Amount>00000470</Amount>
  <Account>0000</Account>
  <RecordID>5</RecordID>
```

```
  </Transaction>
  </Voucher>
  </ABWTransaction>

<b>sample style sheet</b>

<?xml version="1.0" encoding="ISO-8859-1"?>
<xsl:stylesheet
xmlns:xsl="http://www.w3.org/1999/XSL/Transform"
version="1.0">
<xsl:output method="xml" indent="yes"  encoding="uft-
8" omit-xml-declaration="no" />

<xsl:template match="/">
        <ABWTransaction Version="5.4"
xmlns:sql="urn:schemas-microsoft-com:xml-sql">
        <Interface>Bl</Interface>
        <BatchId>YPO</BatchId>
        <Voucher>
            <VoucherType>94</VoucherType>
            <CompanyCode>W5</CompanyCode>
            <VoucherDate><xsl:value-of
select="/ABWTransaction/Voucher/Transaction/Transdate
" /> </VoucherDate>

        <xsl:apply-templates
select="/ABWTransaction/Voucher/Transaction" />

        </Voucher>
      </ABWTransaction>

 </xsl:template>

    <xsl:template match= "Transaction">
        <!--<xsl:for-each
select="/ABWTransaction/Voucher/Transaction">-->
            <xsl:element name="Transaction">
                <xsl:element name="Transtype">
                    <xsl:value-of
select="/ABWTransaction/Voucher/Transaction/TransType
" />
                </xsl:element>
                <xsl:element name="Description">
                    <xsl:value-of
select="/ABWTransaction/Voucher/Transaction/Descripti
on" />
                </xsl:element>
                <!--<xsl:copy-of
select="/ABWTransaction/Voucher/Transaction/Descripti
```

```
on" />-->
                <xsl:element name="TransDate">
                    <xsl:value-of
select="/ABWTransaction/Voucher/Transaction/Transdate
" />
                </xsl:element>

                <xsl:element name="Amounts">
                    <xsl:element name="CurrAmount">
                        <xsl:value-of
select="/ABWTransaction/Voucher/Transaction/CurrAmoun
t"/>
                    </xsl:element>
                    <xsl:element name="Amount">
                        <xsl:value-of
select="/ABWTransaction/Voucher/Transaction/Amount"/>
                    </xsl:element>
                </xsl:element>


                <xsl:element name="GLAnalysis">

                    <xsl:element name="TaxCode">
                        <xsl:value-of
select="/ABWTransaction/Voucher/Transaction/TaxCode"
/>
                    </xsl:element>
                    <xsl:element name="Number1">
                        <xsl:value-of
select="/ABWTransaction/Voucher/Transaction/Number1"
/>
                    </xsl:element>
                    <xsl:element name="InvoiceNo">
                        <xsl:value-of
select="/ABWTransaction/Voucher/Transaction/InvoiceNo
" />
                    </xsl:element>

                    <xsl:element name="Dim7">
                        <xsl:value-of
select="/ABWTransaction/Voucher/Transaction/Dim7"/>
                    </xsl:element>
                    <xsl:element name="Dim6">
                            <xsl:value-of
select="/ABWTransaction/Voucher/Transaction/Dim6"/>
                    </xsl:element>

                    <xsl:element name="Dim1">
                        <xsl:value-of
```

```
select="/ABWTransaction/Voucher/Transaction/Dim1" />
                    </xsl:element>

                    <xsl:element name="Currency">
                        <xsl:value-of
select="/ABWTransaction/Voucher/Transaction/Currency"
/>
                    </xsl:element>
                    <xsl:element name="Account">
                            <xsl:value-of
select="/ABWTransaction/Voucher/Transaction/Account"/
>
                    </xsl:element>
                </xsl:element>
            </xsl:element>


        <!--</xsl:for-each>-->

    </xsl:template>


</xsl:stylesheet>

<b>example output xml</b>

  <?xml version="1.0" encoding="utf-8" ?>
- <ABWTransaction Version="5.4"
xmlns:sql="urn:schemas-microsoft-com:xml-sql">
  <Interface>B1</Interface>
  <BatchId>YPO</BatchId>
- <Voucher>
  <VoucherType>94</VoucherType>
  <CompanyCode>W5</CompanyCode>
  <VoucherDate>2006-04-27T16:54:31.347</VoucherDate>
- <Transaction>
  <Transtype>GL</Transtype>
  <Description>SINGLE HOLE MINI PUNCH</Description>
  <TransDate>2006-04-27T16:54:31.347</TransDate>
- <Amounts>
  <CurrAmount>00000050</CurrAmount>
  <Amount>00000050</Amount>
  </Amounts>
- <GLAnalysis>
  <TaxCode>P2</TaxCode>
  <Number1>000100</Number1>
  <InvoiceNo>714208</InvoiceNo>
  <Dim7 />
  <Dim6 />
```

```
<Dim1 />
<Currency>GBP</Currency>
<Account>0000</Account>
</GLAnalysis>
</Transaction>
- <Transaction>
<Transtype>GL</Transtype>
<Description>SINGLE HOLE MINI PUNCH</Description>
<TransDate>2006-04-27T16:54:31.347</TransDate>
- <Amounts>
<CurrAmount>00000050</CurrAmount>
<Amount>00000050</Amount>
</Amounts>
- <GLAnalysis>
<TaxCode>P2</TaxCode>
<Number1>000100</Number1>
<InvoiceNo>714208</InvoiceNo>
<Dim7 />
<Dim6 />
<Dim1 />
<Currency>GBP</Currency>
<Account>0000</Account>
</GLAnalysis>
</Transaction>
- <Transaction>
<Transtype>GL</Transtype>
<Description>SINGLE HOLE MINI PUNCH</Description>
<TransDate>2006-04-27T16:54:31.347</TransDate>
- <Amounts>
<CurrAmount>00000050</CurrAmount>
<Amount>00000050</Amount>
</Amounts>
- <GLAnalysis>
<TaxCode>P2</TaxCode>
<Number1>000100</Number1>
<InvoiceNo>714208</InvoiceNo>
<Dim7 />
<Dim6 />
<Dim1 />
<Currency>GBP</Currency>
<Account>0000</Account>
</GLAnalysis>
</Transaction>
- <Transaction>
<Transtype>GL</Transtype>
<Description>SINGLE HOLE MINI PUNCH</Description>
<TransDate>2006-04-27T16:54:31.347</TransDate>
- <Amounts>
<CurrAmount>00000050</CurrAmount>
```

```
  <Amount>00000050</Amount>
  </Amounts>
- <GLAnalysis>
  <TaxCode>P2</TaxCode>
  <Number1>000100</Number1>
  <InvoiceNo>714208</InvoiceNo>
  <Dim7 />
  <Dim6 />
  <Dim1 />
  <Currency>GBP</Currency>
  <Account>0000</Account>
  </GLAnalysis>
  </Transaction>
- <Transaction>
  <Transtype>GL</Transtype>
  <Description>SINGLE HOLE MINI PUNCH</Description>
  <TransDate>2006-04-27T16:54:31.347</TransDate>
- <Amounts>
  <CurrAmount>00000050</CurrAmount>
  <Amount>00000050</Amount>
  </Amounts>
- <GLAnalysis>
  <TaxCode>P2</TaxCode>
  <Number1>000100</Number1>
  <InvoiceNo>714208</InvoiceNo>
  <Dim7 />
  <Dim6 />
  <Dim1 />
  <Currency>GBP</Currency>
  <Account>0000</Account>
  </GLAnalysis>
  </Transaction>
  </Voucher>
  </ABWTransaction>
```

How do I accomplish my objective?

A: You need to understand the context within the template. Your xsl:value-of instructions, within the transaction template is using XPath expressions that ignore the context, thereby, getting the first value each time through. Try using this style to take advantage of the correct context:

Code:

```
<xsl:template match= "Transaction">
        <!--<xsl:for-each
```

```
select="/ABWTransaction/Voucher/Transaction">-->
            <Transaction>
                <Transtype>
                    <xsl:value-of select="TransType"
/>
                </Transtype>
```

If you can't get your server's momentum, you should do:

```
<xsl:template match= "Transaction">
    <!--<xsl:for-each
select="/ABWTransaction/Voucher/Transaction">-->
    <xsl:element name="Transaction">
        <xsl:element name="Transtype">
            <xsl:value-of select="TransType" />
        </xsl:element>
        <xsl:element name="Description">
            <xsl:value-of select="Description" />
        </xsl:element>
        <!--<xsl:copy-of
select="/ABWTransaction/Voucher/Transaction/Descripti
on" />-->
        <xsl:element name="TransDate">
            <xsl:value-of select="Transdate" />
        </xsl:element>

        <xsl:element name="Amounts">
            <xsl:element name="CurrAmount">
                <xsl:value-of select="CurrAmount"/>
            </xsl:element>
            <xsl:element name="Amount">
                <xsl:value-of select="Amount"/>
            </xsl:element>
        </xsl:element>

        <xsl:element name="GLAnalysis">
            <xsl:element name="TaxCode">
                <xsl:value-of select="TaxCode" />
            </xsl:element>
            <xsl:element name="Number1">
                <xsl:value-of select="Number1" />
            </xsl:element>
            <xsl:element name="InvoiceNo">
                <xsl:value-of select="InvoiceNo" />
            </xsl:element>
            <xsl:element name="Dim7">
                <xsl:value-of select="Dim7"/>
            </xsl:element>
            <xsl:element name="Dim6">
```

```
                <xsl:value-of select="Dim6"/>
            </xsl:element>
            <xsl:element name="Dim1">
                <xsl:value-of select="Dim1" />
            </xsl:element>
            <xsl:element name="Currency">
                <xsl:value-of select="Currency"/>
            </xsl:element>
            <xsl:element name="Account">
                <xsl:value-of select="Account"/>
            </xsl:element>
        </xsl:element>
    </xsl:element>

        <!--</xsl:for-each>-->

</xsl:template>
```

Question 2: XSL: Including Child Document

I have an XML file that describes data to present in HTML. But one of the possible elements is what we're calling a "super element". It's basically a node that describes another XML file that would need to be included into the HTML presentation.

So, for example, the base XML file is:

```
<?xml version="1.0" encoding="UTF-8"?>
<datapacket>
   <otherdata>
       <dataset>full</dataset>
       <headers>true</headers>
   </otherdata>
   <datarow>
       <element1>1</element1>
       <element2>2</element2>
       <element3>3</element3>
   </datarow>
   <datarow>
       <element1>4</element1>
       <element2>5</element2>
       <element3>6</element3>
```

```
    </datarow>
</datapacket>
```

The other data element is our "super element". Based on its attributes, it determines another XML file to include into this base XML. So the super element might define the inclusion of data2.xml, such that:

```
<?xml version="1.0" encoding="UTF-8"?>
<datapacket>
    <datarow>
        <element1>7</element1>
        <element2>8</element2>
        <element3>9</element3>
    </datarow>
</datapacket>
```

The actual inclusion of the additional XML file is pretty straight forward:

```
<xsl:template match="otherdata">
    <!-- some if/when/test to determine the name of
the additional xml file -->
    <xsl:value-of select="document('data2.xml')" />
</xsl:template>
```

I need to process the entire XML dataset with the stylesheet. If I have:

```
<xsl:template match="datarow">
    :
</xsl:template>
```

It needs to match both the data row elements in the original XML and the data row elements in the data2.xml nodes that just got included. How do I do this?

A: Your XSLT can determine if this <otherdata> exists, and do an:

```
<xsl:apply-templates
select="document('data2.xml')/datapacket" />
```

After that, apply the templates to the elements in the input document.

Question 3: Date Time XSLT

I know there is no direct way to format the date and time but I am having problems getting a template to work.

The date looks like this:
2006-01-17T17:30:00.0000000-08:00

I would like it to look like this:
01/17/2006 5:30 pm

Is there a template that will do this?

A: Yes, there is. Just let XSL do all the labor.

```
<!-- variable name: given, alias x -->
<xsl:variable name="given" select="'2006-01-
17T17:30:00.0000000-08:00'" />
<xsl:variable name="y" select="substring-
before($given,'T')" />
<xsl:variable name="CCYY" select="substring-
before($y,'-')" />
<xsl:variable name="tmp" select="substring-
after($y,'-')" />
<xsl:variable name="MM" select="substring-
before($tmp,'-')" />
<xsl:variable name="DD" select="substring-
after($tmp,'-')" />
<xsl:variable name="z" select="substring-
after($given,'T')" />
<xsl:variable name="hh" select="substring-
before($z,':')" />
<xsl:variable name="tmp2" select="substring-
after($z,':')" />
<xsl:variable name="mm" select="substring-
before($tmp2,':')" />
<xsl:variable name="tmp3" select="substring-
after($tmp2,':')" />
<xsl:variable name="hh_norm">
    <xsl:choose>
        <xsl:when test="$hh &gt; 12">
            <xsl:value-of select="$hh - 12" />
        </xsl:when>
```

```
        <xsl:otherwise>
            <xsl:value-of select="$hh" />
        </xsl:otherwise>
    </xsl:choose>
</xsl:variable>
<xsl:variable name="sffx">
    <xsl:choose>
        <xsl:when test="$hh &gt; 12">
            <xsl:value-of select="'pm'" />
        </xsl:when>
        <xsl:otherwise>
            <xsl:value-of select="'am'" />
        </xsl:otherwise>
    </xsl:choose>
</xsl:variable>
<xsl:variable name="mm_norm" select="$mm" />
<xsl:variable name="result"
select="concat($MM,'/',$DD,'/',$CCYY,'
',$hh_norm,':',$mm_norm,' ',$sffx)" />
<!-- display result here -->
<xsl:value-of select="$result" />
```

You might have some format number to do in order to improve fixed length integer according to your needs.

Question 4: Find and Replace in XSL

We have a small shipping program where we can write custom invoices in XSL. I have a field that is pulled in at the end of the invoice: Order Notes. This will contain special notes written by the customer. Sometimes the data in this field contains the phrase "Buyer Notes:" before the customer data, but sometimes it doesn't. If the data contains "Buyer Notes:" I don't want it pulled into the invoice.

We had a piece of code like this:

```
<xsl:template name="outputPageFooter">
<br> </br>
<table id="orderdetails" cellspacing="0">

      <tr class="header">
        <td>Special Instructions</td>
        </tr>
```

```
        <tr class="orderitem">
        <td><xsl:value-of select="substring-
after(//Order/Notes, 'Buyer notes:')" /></td>
        </tr>

</table>
<br> </br>
```

However, we were finding that sometimes the order notes were missing altogether when the invoice printed. Do I need a more sophisticated statement that only removes the text "Buyer's Notes:" when it is actually in the field?

A: Try doing this:

```
><td><xsl:value-of select="substring-
after(//Order/Notes, 'Buyer notes:')" /></td>
```

Maybe, replace it with this:

```
<td><xsl:choose>
    <xsl:when test="contains(//Order/Notes,'Buyer
notes:')">
        <xsl:value-of select="substring-
after(//Order/Notes,'Buyer notes:')" />
    </xsl:when>
    <xsl:otherwise>
        <xsl:value-of select="//Order/Notes" />
    </xsl:otherwise>
</xsl:choose></td>
```

Question 5: XSL Transformation

I have an XML document with the following form:

```
<ArrayOfSomething>
  <Something>
    <MyElement
xmlns="http://www.tempuri.org/>somevalue</MyElement>
  </Something>
  <Something>
    <MyElement
xmlns="http://www.tempuri.org/>anothervalue</MyElemen
t>
  </Something>
</ArrayOfSomething>
```

and an XSL transformation of the form:

```
<xsl:template match="ArrayOfSomething">
  <xsl:for-each select="Something">
    <xsl:value-of select="MyElement" />
    <xsl:text>statictext</xsl:text>
  </xsl:for-each>
</xsl:template>
```

When I run this transformation, all I'm getting is the static text element. It doesn't seem to be picking up the MyElement element. I know this has something to do with the XML's attribute because when I remove it the transform works. I'm trying to address this separately as the source XML doc is the serialization of a complex type returned from a web service.

What expression could I use in the value-of element to pick up the element's value?

A: Declare the namespace in XSL with a name freely given to the default namespace of the set of elements. Then to match them, match them with a fully qualified name with such called namespace prefixed to them.

```
<xsl:stylesheet version="1.0"
xmlns:xsl="http://www.w3.org/1999/XSL/Transform"
    xmlns:dfns="http://www.tempuri.org/">
```

```
<xsl:template match="ArrayOfSomething">
  <xsl:for-each select="Something">
    <xsl:value-of select="dfns:MyElement" />
    <xsl:text>statictext</xsl:text>
  </xsl:for-each>
</xsl:template>
</xsl:stylesheet>
```

Question 6: Write XML Element Into Textbox With XSLT

I'm using XSLT to format an XML document but I want to write some of the XML into HTML form controls. For example, I'd like a textbox to contain the data from one of the XML elements. It won't let me do this:

```
<input type="text" id="whatever" value="<xsl:value-of
select="RESPONSE"/>" />
```

Is there a better way to achieve this?

A: You can try doing it this way:

```
><input type="text" id="whatever" value="<xsl:value-
of select="RESPONSE"/>" />
```

It is about this if RESPONSE is the correct match.

```
<input>
    <xsl:attribute name="type">text</xsl:attribute>
    <xsl:attribute name="id">whatever</xsl:attribute>
    <xsl:attribute name="value"><xsl:value-of
select="RESPONSE" /></xsl:attribute>
</input>
```

Question 7: Bad XSL Transformation in Firefox

When I open the following XML file in Internet Explorer 6, everything is formatted neatly into a table as desired. However, when I view the same XML file in Firefox the header_record and table all appear on one line appropriately colored by the style set at the top of the style sheet. What is the reason for this?

Here is my source code example of XSL:

```
<?xml version="1.0" encoding="UTF-8"?>
 <xsl:stylesheet version="1.0"
xmlns:xsl="http://www.w3.org/1999/XSL/Transform"
xmlns:fo="http://www.w3.org/1999/XSL/Format">
  <xsl:template match="/">
   <html xmlns="http://www.w3.org/1999/xhtml">
    <head>
     <style type="text/css">
      h2
      {
       background-color: #000000;
       color: #FFFFCC;
       text-align: center;
      }

      h3
      {
       background: #FFFFCC;
       text-align: center;
      }

      h4
      {
       background: #FFCC99;
       text-align: center;
      }

      table
      {
       border-color: #000000 #000000 #000000 #000000;
       border-spacing: 2;
       border-width: 2;
       padding: 2;
      }

      td.heading
```

```
        {
         background: #0000CC;
         color: #FFFFFF;
         font-weight: bold;
        }

        td.total
        {
         font-weight: bold;
        }

        td
        {
         background: #CCCCFF;
        }
       </style>
       <title>Network Data File</title>
      </head>
      <body>
        <h2>Network Data File</h2>
        <xsl:apply-templates
select="network_data_file/header_record"/>
      </body>
    </html>
   </xsl:template>
   <xsl:template match="header_record">
    <h3>Header Record</h3>
    <table border="1">
     <tr>
      <td class="heading"> Network Name </td>
      <td class="heading"> State Name </td>
     </tr>
     <tr>
      <td><xsl:value-of select="netName"/></td>
      <td><xsl:value-of select="stateName"/></td>
     </tr>
    </table>
   </xsl:template>
  </xsl:stylesheet>
example.xml
<?xml version="1.0" encoding="ISO-8859-1"?>
<?xml-stylesheet type="text/xsl" href="example.xsl" ?
>
<network_data_file
xmlns:xsi="http://www.w3.org/2001/XMLSchema-instance"
xsi:noNamespaceSchemaLocation="network_data_file.xsd"
>
 <header_record>
  <netName>Example</netName>
```

```
  <stateName>On</stateName>
 </header_record>
</network_data_file>
```

A: The reason is that the vocabulary is unknown to the namespace the parser is trying to interpret when it reads the template apart.

To illustrate the mechanism, I can show you how to make cases out of your example.xls. Then you may understand the issue better.

1. The realization of example.xls which works in IE and fails in moz/ff.; this you have shown us.

2. The realization of example.xls which works in moz/ff and fails in IE.

```
<?xml version="1.0" encoding="UTF-8"?>
<xsl:stylesheet version="1.0"
    xmlns:xsl="http://www.w3.org/1999/XSL/Transform"
    xmlns:fo="http://www.w3.org/1999/XSL/Format"
    xmlns:html="http://www.w3.org/1999/xhtml">
    <xsl:template match="/">
        <html xmlns="http://www.w3.org/1999/xhtml">
        <head>
        <style type="text/css">
        h2{background-color: #000000;color:
#FFFFCC;text-align: center;}
        h3{background: #FFFFCC;text-align:center;}
        h4{background: #FFCC99;text-align: center;}
        table{border-color: #000000 #000000 #000000
#000000;border-spacing: 2; border-width: 2;padding:
2;}
        td.heading{background: #0000CC;color:
#FFFFFF;font-weight: bold;}
        td.total{font-weight: bold;}
        td{background: #CCCCFF;}
        </style>
        <title>Network Data File</title>
        </head>
        <body>
            <h2>Network Data File</h2>
            <h3>Header Record</h3>
        <xsl:apply-templates
select="network_data_file/header_record" />
        </body>
```

```
        </html>
    </xsl:template>

    <xsl:template
match="network_data_file/header_record">
        <html:table border="1">
            <html:tr>
            <html:td class="heading"> Network Name
</html:td>
            <html:td class="heading"> State Name
</html:td>
            </html:tr>
            <html:tr>
                <html:td><xsl:value-of
select="netName" /></html:td>
                <html:td><xsl:value-of
select="stateName" /></html:td>
            </html:tr>
        </html:table>
    </xsl:template>
</xsl:stylesheet>
```

3. The realization of example.xls which works both in moz/ff and in IE.

```
<?xml version="1.0" encoding="UTF-8"?>
<xsl:stylesheet version="1.0"
    xmlns:xsl="http://www.w3.org/1999/XSL/Transform"
    xmlns:fo="http://www.w3.org/1999/XSL/Format"
    xmlns="http://www.w3.org/1999/xhtml">
    <xsl:template match="/">
        <!-- is not really matter
        <html xmlns="http://www.w3.org/1999/xhtml">
        -->
        <html>
        <head>
        <style type="text/css">
        h2{background-color: #000000;color:
#FFFFCC;text-align: center;}
        h3{background: #FFFFCC;text-align:center;}
        h4{background: #FFCC99;text-align: center;}
        table{border-color: #000000 #000000 #000000
#000000;border-spacing: 2; border-width: 2;padding:
2;}
        td.heading{background: #0000CC;color:
#FFFFFF;font-weight: bold;}
        td.total{font-weight: bold;}
        td{background: #CCCCFF;}
```

```
        </style>
        <title>Network Data File</title>
        </head>
        <body>
            <h2>Network Data File</h2>
            <h3>Header Record</h3>
        <xsl:apply-templates
select="network_data_file/header_record" />
        </body>
        </html>
    </xsl:template>

    <xsl:template
match="network_data_file/header_record">
        <table border="1">
            <tr>
            <td class="heading"> Network Name </td>
            <td class="heading"> State Name </td>
            </tr>
            <tr>
                <td><xsl:value-of select="netName"
/></td>
                <td><xsl:value-of select="stateName"
/></td>
            </tr>
        </table>
    </xsl:template>
</xsl:stylesheet>
```

With these variations, it will better articulate the problem involved.

Question 8: XSL Drop Down Box

I have a tag <pregnant>. I want to create a drop down box with three options in HTML: "blank", Yes, and No. Depending on what is in the tag of <pregnant>, I'd like to have one of the three selected. How can I do this?

A: You can do it as follows:

```
<select name="pregnant">
  <option value=""/>
  <option value="Yes">
    <xsl:if test="preganant = 'Yes'">
      <xsl:attribute
name="selected">selected</xsl:attribute>
    </xsl:if>
  </option>
  <option value="No">
    <xsl:if test="preganant = 'No'">
      <xsl:attribute
name="selected">selected</xsl:attribute>
    </xsl:if>
  </option>
</select>
```

Question 9: Simple Problem, Spaces (xsl)

I have an address in the XML that's divided into parts. In the XSL :

```
<xsl:value-of select="streetNumber"
/><xsl:text> </xsl:text>
<xsl:value-of select="streetName" />,<br />
<xsl:value-of sel... etc etc
```

The problem is that not all the entries have a streetNumber value, but the " " is always going to add a space before the streetName. Is there any solution for this?

A: This would be a better code set for your problem.

```
<xsl:if test="string-length(streetNumber)">
  <xsl:value-of select="streetNumber" />
  <xsl:text> </xsl:text>
</xsl:if>
```

Question 10: Putting XSL into HTML

Is there any way to put XSL into an HTML tag? In my XSL file I have a link to an image file:

```
<img src="?Image?.jpg" />
```

As there are no links to images in the XML, I want to use an ID:

```
 <venue venueID="?Image?">
```

I learned from somebody how to make venueID dynamic. This way I can have a different image each time it's called. I tried putting the XSL I know directly into the image tag but it made the XSL invalid.

A: You can use curly brackets to denote an XPATH expression:

```
<img src="{$venueID}.jpg"/>;
```

Question 11: XSL to Create Array

Is there a way to create an array similar to JavaScript in XSL? Is there a similar way to store data like an array and access it?

A: You can store data in a separate XML file, then reference it with document() function. You can also store a node set in a variable. To create a node set inside a variable, do the following:

```
<xsl:variable name="myArray">
  <elem>1</elem>
  <elem>2</elem>
  <elem>3</elem>
  <elem>4</elem>
  <elem>5</elem>
</xsl:variable>
```

Depending on what version of XSL you're using, you'll probably need to use an extension function -- nodeset() -- to deal with the result tree fragment. The MSXSL extension can be used as follows:

```
xmlns:msxsl="urn:schemas-microsoft-com:xslt"
Now you can refer to the array (eg 3rd element) as
follows:

<xsl:value-of
select="msxsl:nodeset($myArray)/elem[3]"/>;
```

Question 12: Inserting XML Date in IMG Tag

The following code returns a number. The number is the name of a picture (i.e. 32.gif, 33.gif, etc)

```
<xsl:value-of select="//yweather:condition/@code"/>
```

How can I insert the number in the IMG tag so it would read as follows:

```
<img
src="http://us.i1.yimg.com/us.yimg.com/i/us/we/52/INS
ERT NUMBER HERE FROM XML.gif" />
```

A: You can try the following code:

```
<?xml version="1.0" ?>
<xsl:stylesheet
xmlns:xsl="http://www.w3.org/1999/XSL/Transform"
version="1.0"
xmlns:yweather="http://xml.weather.yahoo.com/ns/rss/1
.0">
<xsl:output method="xml" encoding="iso-8859-1" omit-
xml-declaration="yes" indent="yes"/>
<xsl:template match="*">

  <tr><td colspan="2" align="center"
class="evt"><b><xsl:value-of
select="//yweather:location/@city"/></b></td></tr>
  <tr>
    <td align="center" class="evt">
      <img
src="http://us.i1.yimg.com/us.yimg.com/i/us/we/52/32.
gif" /><br/>
      <xsl:value-of
select="//yweather:condition/@text"/><br/>
      <xsl:value-of
select="//yweather:condition/@temp"/><xsl:text
disable-output-
escaping="yes">&amp;deg;</xsl:text><br/>
    </td>
    <td align="right" valign="bottom" class="evt">
      <table align="center" cellpadding="0"
cellspacing="0">
      <xsl:for-each select="//yweather:forecast">
```

```
         <tr>
           <td><xsl:value-of select="@day"/></td>
           <td width="5"></td>
           <td><xsl:value-of select="@high"/></td>
           <td width="10" align="center">/</td>
           <td><xsl:value-of select="@low"/></td>
         </tr>
       </xsl:for-each>
       </table>
     </td>
   </tr>
   <tr><td colspan="2" height="5"
class="evt"></td></tr>
   <tr><td colspan="2" align="center"
class="evt"><font size="-3" color="#999999">Sunset is
at <xsl:value-of
select="//yweather:astronomy/@sunset"/></font></td></
tr>

</xsl:template>
</xsl:stylesheet>
```

You also need curly brackets:

```
<img
src="http://us.i1.yimg.com/us.yimg.com/i/us/we/52/{//
yweather:condition/@code}.gif" />
```

Avoid using the double backslash // as it will search every node in the tree and can be very slow with large documents. Always specify the full path when you know it.

Question 13: XML/XSL Loading Time Problem

I built an XML database from where I extract data to show in an HTML page. The problem is that when I test the loading time local on my pc, this goes very fast, but as soon as I upload the site to my host the loading time takes up to 5–10 seconds.

This is the XML file -> http://www.basisdeco.nl/vloerendb.xml;

This is one of the XSL files -> http://www.basisdeco.nl/parador/witeiken.xsl;

This is the html file that extracts the data -> http://www.basisdeco.nl/parador/parador.htm;

I would like to know what's wrong? Is something looping? How can I make the loading time faster?

A: The best way to improve the loading time is to transform the server-side. This would speed things up considerably. At the moment, the browser has to load the HTML completely, then load the XML and XSL, and then do the transform.

It should look like this:

```
<SCRIPT type="text/javascript">
var xml = new ActiveXObject("Microsoft.XMLDOM")
        xml.async = false
        xml.load("../vloerendb.xml")
</SCRIPT>
```

This goes to the head of the HTML file instead of loading the XML file several times. And to transform the data on the server side you need to use some sort of server-side script like ASP, JSP, Coldfusion, CGI, etc.

Question 14: XSLT Has Nested Loops

Can XSLT have nested loops? I have this XML file:

```
  <?xml version="1.0" ?>
- <ASSORTMENT>
-   <FIXEDASSORTMENT>
     <DESCRIPTION>NACS SMALL ASSORTMENT</DESCRIPTION>

      <COST>0.00</COST>
      <ITEMNO>954469N</ITEMNO>
-     <ITEMS>
       <ITEM>$4.99 JUV ASST</ITEM>
       <ITEM>$6.99 FIC ASST</ITEM>
       <ITEM>$6.99 NON FIC ASST</ITEM>
       <ITEM>$9.99 HOUSE/HOME ASST</ITEM>
      </ITEMS>
    </FIXEDASSORTMENT>
-   <FIXEDASSORTMENT>
     <DESCRIPTION>NACS MEDIUM
ASSORTMENT</DESCRIPTION>
     <COST>0.00</COST>
     <ITEMNO>954470N</ITEMNO>
-    <ITEMS>
      <ITEM>$4.99 JUV ASST</ITEM>
      <ITEM>$6.99 FIC ASST</ITEM>
      <ITEM>$6.99 NON FIC ASST</ITEM>
      <ITEM>$9.99 HOUSE/HOME ASST</ITEM>
     </ITEMS>
    </FIXEDASSORTMENT>
.
.
```

And this is my XSLT style sheet:

```
<xsl:stylesheet version="1.0"
xmlns:xsl="http://www.w3.org/1999/XSL/Transform"
xmlns:msxsl="urn:schemas-microsoft-com:xslt"
xmlns:user="urn:my-scripts">
    <xsl:template match="ASSORTMENT">
        <table width="90%" border="0" cellSpacing="0"
cellPadding="0">
            <xsl:for-each select="FIXEDASSORTMENT">
                <table width="70%" border="0"
cellSpacing="0" cellPadding="0">
                    <tr bgcolor="LIGHTBLUE">
                        <td width="100"><font
```

```
face="Arial,Helvetica,sans-serif" size="2"
color="black"><b><xsl:value-of
select="ITEMNO"/></b></font></td>
                        <td><font
face="Arial,Helvetica,sans-serif" size="2"
color="black"><b><xsl:value-of
select="DESCRIPTION"/></b></font></td>
                        <td width="100"
align="RIGHT"><font face="Arial,Helvetica,sans-serif"
size="2" color="black"><b><xsl:value-of
select="format-number(COST,
'$#,##0.00')"/></b></font></td>
                    </tr>
                    <xsl:for-each
select="/ASSORTMENT/FIXEDASSORTMENT/ITEMS">
                        <tr bgcolor="LIGHTYELLOW">
                            <td><font
face="Arial,Helvetica,sans-serif" size="2"
color="black">  </font></td>
                            <td colspan="2"><font
face="Arial,Helvetica,sans-serif" size="2"
color="black"><xsl:value-of
select="ITEM"/></font></td>
                        </tr>
                    </xsl:for-each>
                </table>

                <br/>
            </xsl:for-each>
        </table>
    </xsl:template>
</xsl:stylesheet>
```

No matter what I do, I keep getting results like this:

```
954469N   NACS SMALL ASSORTMENT       $0.00
          $4.99 JUV ASST
          $4.99 JUV ASST
          $4.99 JUV ASST
          $4.99 JUV ASST

954469N   NACS MEDUIMASSORTMENT       $0.00
          $4.99 JUV ASST
          $4.99 JUV ASST
          $4.99 JUV ASST
          $4.99 JUV ASST
```

What did I do wrong?

A: Try changing the codes to:

```
<xsl:for-each
select="/ASSORTMENT/FIXEDASSORTMENT/ITEMS"> to:

<xsl:for-each select="ITEMS">
```

You want the inner for-each to iterate over the ITEMS in the context of the node selected by the outer for-each.

If Pressed Submit too quickly, then you need to change to:

```
<xsl:value-of select="ITEM"/> to:

<xsl:value-of select="."/>
```

To select the value of the current node within the context of the inner for-each, then it would have the following:

```
 <?xml version="1.0" ?>
- <ASSORTMENT>
- <FIXEDASSORTMENT>
  <DESCRIPTION>NACS SMALL ASSORTMENT</DESCRIPTION>
  <COST>0.00</COST>
  <ITEMNO>954469N</ITEMNO>
- <ITEMS>
- <ITEM>
  <ITEM>$4.99 JUV ASST</ITEM>
  </ITEM>
- <ITEM>
  <ITEM>$6.99 FIC ASST</ITEM>
  </ITEM>
- <ITEM>
  <ITEM>$6.99 NON FIC ASST</ITEM>
  </ITEM>
- <ITEM>
  <ITEM>$9.99 HOUSE/HOME ASST</ITEM>
  </ITEM>
  </ITEMS>
  <EXIST>TRUE</EXIST>
  </FIXEDASSORTMENT>
- <FIXEDASSORTMENT>
  <DESCRIPTION>NACS MEDIUM ASSORTMENT</DESCRIPTION>
  <COST>0.00</COST>
  <ITEMNO>954470N</ITEMNO>
- <ITEMS>[b][color red]
```

```
- <ITEM>
  <ITEM>$4.99 JUV ASST</ITEM>
  </ITEM>
- <ITEM>
  <ITEM>$6.99 FIC ASST</ITEM>
  </ITEM>
- <ITEM>
  <ITEM>$6.99 NON FIC ASST</ITEM>
  </ITEM>
- <ITEM>
  <ITEM>$9.99 HOUSE/HOME ASST</ITEM>
  </ITEM>[b][color red]
  </ITEMS>
  <EXIST>TRUE</EXIST>
  </FIXEDASSORTMENT>
.
.
.
```

and my XSLT as:

```
<xsl:stylesheet version="1.0"
xmlns:xsl="http://www.w3.org/1999/XSL/Transform"
xmlns:msxsl="urn:schemas-microsoft-com:xslt"
xmlns:user="urn:my-scripts">
    <xsl:template match="/">
        <table width="90%" border="0" cellSpacing="0"
cellPadding="0">
            <xsl:for-each
select="ASSORTMENT/FIXEDASSORTMENT">
                <table width="70%" border="0"
cellSpacing="0" cellPadding="0">
                    <tr bgcolor="#99CC99">
                        <td width="100"><font
face="Arial,Helvetica,sans-serif"
size="2"><b><xsl:value-of
select="ITEMNO"/></b></font></td>
                        <td><font
face="Arial,Helvetica,sans-serif"
size="2"><b><xsl:value-of
select="DESCRIPTION"/></b></font></td>
                        <td width="100"
align="RIGHT"><font face="Arial,Helvetica,sans-serif"
size="2" color="Red"><b><xsl:value-of select="format-
number(COST, '$#,##0.00')"/></b></font></td>
                    </tr>
                    <xsl:for-each
select="ITEMS/ITEM">
```

```
                              <tr bgcolor="LIGHTYELLOW">
                                  <td><font
face="Arial,Helvetica,sans-serif" size="2"
color="black">  </font></td>
                                  <td colspan="2"><font
face="Arial,Helvetica,sans-serif" size="2"
color="black"><xsl:value-of
select="ITEM"/></font></td>
                              </tr>
                          </xsl:for-each>
                          <tr bgcolor="LIGHTYELLOW">
                              <td colspan="3"><font
face="Arial,Helvetica,sans-serif" size="1"
color="black">  </font></td>
                          </tr>
                      </table>
                          <xsl:if test="string-
length(EXIST)">

                          <IMG
src="images/btn_addItemsToCart.gif" border="0"/>
                          </xsl:if>

                      <br/><font
face="Arial,Helvetica,sans-serif" size="1"
color="black">  </font>
                      <br/>
                  </xsl:for-each>
              </table>
          </xsl:template>
</xsl:stylesheet>
```

It's now working great. Another way of doing this is as follows. The entire style sheet is derived from your original post, modified as indicated, with my error corrected.

```
<xsl:stylesheet version="1.0"
xmlns:xsl="http://www.w3.org/1999/XSL/Transform"
xmlns:msxsl="urn:schemas-microsoft-com:xslt"
xmlns:user="urn:my-scripts">
    <xsl:template match="ASSORTMENT">
        <table width="90%" border="0" cellSpacing="0"
cellPadding="0">
            <xsl:for-each select="FIXEDASSORTMENT">
                <table width="70%" border="0"
cellSpacing="0" cellPadding="0">
                    <tr bgcolor="LIGHTBLUE">
                        <td width="100"><font
```

```
face="Arial,Helvetica,sans-serif" size="2"
color="black"><b><xsl:value-of
select="ITEMNO"/></b></font></td>
                            <td><font
face="Arial,Helvetica,sans-serif" size="2"
color="black"><b><xsl:value-of
select="DESCRIPTION"/></b></font></td>
                            <td width="100"
align="RIGHT"><font face="Arial,Helvetica,sans-serif"
size="2" color="black"><b><xsl:value-of
select="format-number(COST,
'$#,##0.00')"/></b></font></td>
                        </tr>
                        <xsl:for-each
select="ITEMS/ITEM">
                            <tr bgcolor="LIGHTYELLOW">
                                <td><font
face="Arial,Helvetica,sans-serif" size="2"
color="black">  </font></td>
                                <td colspan="2"><font
face="Arial,Helvetica,sans-serif" size="2"
color="black"><xsl:value-of select="."/></font></td>
                            </tr>
                        </xsl:for-each>
                    </table>

                    <br/>
                </xsl:for-each>
            </table>
        </xsl:template>
</xsl:stylesheet>
```

I will again call your attention to the mechanism of “xsl:for-each”. The select="ITEMS" says “please iterate of all the nodes named ITEMS within my current context of FIXEDASSORTMENT”. Since each FIXEDASSORTMENT had exactly one ITEM node, it did not do what was needed, which is to iterate over the node set of all ITEM subordinate to ITEMS within my current context of FIXEDASSORTMENT.

Question 15: Cannot View XML Input Using XSL Style Sheet

I have a code that elicits an error message. The error message states that a semi-colon is expected and that an error occurred in processing my resource file. The message also retrieves the first URL line as to where the problem is occurring.

```
<FL:smarttaglist xmlns:FL="urn:schemas-microsoft-com:smarttags:list">
   <FL:name>Related Data</FL:name>
   <FL:description>Shows Data</FL:description>
   <FL:updateable>false</FL:updateable>
   <FL:updatefrequency>10080</FL:updatefrequency>
   <FL:autoupdate>true</FL:autoupdate>
   <FL:smarttag type="urn:schemas-microsoft-com:office:smarttags#States">
      <FL:caption>Insitutional Shareholder Data</FL:caption>
      <FL:terms>
         <FL:termlist>"Sports", "Hsitory" </FL:termlist>
      </FL:terms>
      <FL:actions>
          <FL:action id="Sports">
            <FL:caption>My Sports</FL:caption>
            <FL:url>"http://session.rservices.com/data/IcomServer?component=institutions&root=Soccer"</FL:url>
      </FL:action>
         <FL:action id="Info">
           <FL:caption>More Info</FL:caption>
           <FL:url>www.soccernet.com</FL:url>
      </FL:action>
   </FL:actions>
   </FL:smarttag>
</FL:smarttaglist>
```

How do I resolve this?

A: “The” & “char” is illegal. Try replacing it with '&' and try this code:

```
<FL:url>"http://session.rservices.com/data/IcomServer?component=institutions&amp;root=Soccer"</FL:url>
```

Question 16: Separating XML Data–XSLT

I've got an XML data structure as follows:

```
<entry>
      <name>New Entry</name>

       <dataSet1>
            <showingResults>1-5</showingResults
                 <result>
                      <docTitle>April 2005</docTitle>
                      <docPath>c:/april2005.pdf</docP
ath>
                 </result>
                 <result>
                      <docTitle>March 2005</docTitle>
                      <docPath>c:/march2005.pdf</docP
ath>
                 </result>
                 ...more <result> entries
       </dataset1>

       <dataset2>
                ... same structure as above,
different values
       </dataset2>
</entry>
```

Can I create hyperlinks to the different datasets through XSLT? For example, my XSLT generates 2 hyperlinks, one for dataset1 and one for dataset2. When I click a hyperlink, it changes a div or iframe to display the relevant set. Is it possible before I attempt to delve into JavaScript?

A: It is possible for XSLT to generate the hyperlinks, but you'll need to use JavaScript to actually hide/show the divs. See the code below:

```
<?xml version="1.0" encoding="ISO-8859-1"?>
<xsl:stylesheet version="1.0"
xmlns:xsl="http://www.w3.org/1999/XSL/Transform">
  <xsl:template match="/">
    <html>
      <head>
```

```
        <title>Test</title>
        <script type="text/javascript">
  function show(dataSet)
  {
    for (var i = 1; i &lt; <xsl:value-of
select="count(entry/dataSet) + 1"/>; i++)
    {
      document.getElementById("dataSet" +
i).style.display = "none";
    }
    document.getElementById("dataSet" +
dataSet).style.display = "block";
  }
        </script>
      </head>
      <body>
        <xsl:apply-templates select="entry"/>
      </body>
    </html>
  </xsl:template>
  <xsl:template match="entry">
    <h1>
      <xsl:value-of select="name"/>
    </h1>
    <ul>
      <xsl:apply-templates select="dataSet"
mode="links"/>
    </ul>
    <xsl:apply-templates select="dataSet"
mode="divs"/>
  </xsl:template>
  <xsl:template match="dataSet" mode="links">
    <li>
      <a href="#"
onclick="javascript:show({position()});">
        <xsl:value-of select="concat('Show dataSet ',
position())"/>
      </a>
    </li>
  </xsl:template>
  <xsl:template match="dataSet" mode="divs">
    <div id="dataSet{position()}" style="display:
none;">
      <h2>
        <xsl:value-of select="concat('Showing
results: ', showingResults)"/>
      </h2>
      <ul>
        <xsl:apply-templates select="result"/>
```

```
      </ul>
    </div>
  </xsl:template>
  <xsl:template match="result">
    <li>
      <a href="{docPath}">
        <xsl:value-of select="docTitle"/>
      </a>
    </li>
  </xsl:template>
</xsl:stylesheet>
```

Question 17: MotleyFool RDF Transform With XSL Problem

I'm attempting to simply parse the RDF file provided by financial website MotleyFool, http://www.fool.co.uk/scripts/rss_headlines.asp, to have the "item" contents appear in a <ul> in the form:

```
<ul>
<li><a href="link">title</a</li>
...
...
</ul>
```

How can I do this correctly?

A: This is the RDF file from the website:

<?xml version="1.0"?>
<!--Usage of this file constitutes agreement with The Motley Fool UK terms of use found at http://www.fool.co.uk/help/headlines/headlines.htm#tos. Please direct questions to headlines@fool.co.uk-->
<rdf:RDF xmlns:rdf="http://www.w3.org/1999/02/22-rdf-syntax-ns#" xmlns="http://my.netscape.com/rdf/simple/0.9/">
<channel>
<title>The Motley Fool UK</title>
<link>http://www.fool.co.uk</link>
<description>To Educate, Amuse, and Enrich</description>
</channel>

```
  <image>
    <title>The Motley Fool UK</title>
    <url>http://www.fool.co.uk/art/buttons/88x31uk.gif</url>
    <link>http://www.fool.co.uk/</link>
  </image>
  <item>
    <title>Comment: The Next 12,100% Return</title>
    <link>http://www.fool.co.uk/news/comment/2005/c05083
1c.htm?ref=foolwatch</link>
  </item>
  <item>
    <title>Comment: Don&#39;t Fall For This Card
Trick!</title>
    <link>http://www.fool.co.uk/news/comment/2005/c05083
1d.htm?ref=foolwatch</link>
  </item>
  <item>
    <title>Comment: High Yield Tips From Top City
Investors</title>
    <link>http://www.fool.co.uk/news/comment/2005/c05083
1b.htm?ref=foolwatch</link>
  </item>
  <item>
    <title>U.S. Shares: Here&#39;s Your Hammer</title>
    <link>http://www.fool.co.uk/stockideas/2005/si050831.ht
m?ref=foolwatch</link>
  </item>
  <item>
    <title>Fool School: Balance Sheet Basics: Part I</title>
    <link>http://www.fool.co.uk/school/2005/sch050831.htm?
ref=foolwatch</link>
  </item>
  <item>
    <title>Comment: Create A Comfort Zone Of Cash</title>
    <link>http://www.fool.co.uk/news/comment/2005/c05083
0a.htm?ref=foolwatch</link>
  </item>
  <item>
    <title>Comment: Home Loans From Heaven - And
Hell!</title>
    <link>http://www.fool.co.uk/news/comment/2005/c05083
0d.htm?ref=foolwatch</link>
  </item>
  <item>
```

```
    <title>Comment: How To Spot A Scam</title>
    <link>http://www.fool.co.uk/news/comment/2005/c05083
0e.htm?ref=foolwatch</link>
  </item>
  <item>
    <title>Comment: Why You Shouldn&#39;t Keep Your Debts
Secret</title>
    <link>http://www.fool.co.uk/news/comment/2005/c05083
0c.htm?ref=foolwatch</link>
  </item>
  <item>
    <title>Fool&#39;s Eye View: Your Two-Minute Financial
Health Check</title>
    <link>http://www.fool.co.uk/news/foolseyeview/2005/fev0
50830c.htm?ref=foolwatch</link>
  </item>
  <item>
    <title>Qualiport: The Best Customers For Your
Shares</title>
    <link>http://www.fool.co.uk/qualiport/2005/qualiport050
830.htm?ref=foolwatch</link>
  </item>
</rdf:RDF>
```

If you're having a default namespace problem with the help of the FAQ and Googling on default namespace RDF issues, I found http://www.xslt.com/html/xsl-list/2002-04/msg00114.html which, combined with the FAQ, ironed out the issues. The resulting XSL is this:

```
<?xml version="1.0" encoding="ISO-8859-1"?>

<xsl:stylesheet version="1.0"
    xmlns:xsl="http://www.w3.org/1999/XSL/Transform"
    xmlns:rdf="http://www.w3.org/1999/02/22-rdf-
syntax-ns#"
    xmlns:fool="http://my.netscape.com/rdf/simple/0.9
/">

<xsl:template match="rdf:RDF">
<span class="boxList">
<ul>
    <xsl:apply-templates select="fool:item" />
</ul>
</span>
```

```
</xsl:template>

<xsl:template match="fool:item">
    <li> <a href="{fool:link}"><xsl:value-of
select="fool:title"/></a></li>
</xsl:template>
</xsl:stylesheet>
```

Question 18: White Spaces in XSL

I'm looking for ways to replace all white spaces with a character ("_") in an attribute of an element with XSL. Here is an example in original XML document:

```
    <doc   name="ela  yil  eliminate  white spaces">
```

and I want to change it using XSL to:

```
    <doc   name="ela_yil_eliminate_white_spaces">
```

How can I make this work?

A: You can try doing this:

```
<?xml version="1.0"?>
<xsl:stylesheet version="1.0"
xmlns:xsl="http://www.w3.org/1999/XSL/Transform">
  <xsl:template match="node()">
    <xsl:copy>
      <xsl:apply-templates select="@*|node()"/>
    </xsl:copy>
  </xsl:template>
  <xsl:template match="@*">
    <xsl:attribute name="{name(.)}">
      <xsl:value-of select="translate(.,  ' ',  '_')"/>
    </xsl:attribute>
  </xsl:template>
</xsl:stylesheet>
```

To eliminate white spaces, try doing the following.

For example in original XML document, there exists:

```
<doc  name="ela  yil  eliminate  white spaces">
```

and I want to change it using XSL to:

```
<doc  name="elayileliminatewhitespaces">
```

You can use the same thing, but put <xsl:value-of select="translate(., ' ', '')"/>

Question 19: Creating a Variable in XSL

I am trying to loop through my XML file and create a variable "count". The code I have is:

```
<xsl:for-each select="hotel/images/image">
<a href="javascript:void(0);"
onClick="slideshow('slideshow.php?id=4110&count=count
')" target="_blank">
<img src="{ThumbnailURL}" border="0"/>
</a>
</xsl:for-each>
```

What I need to do is to assign count to an incrementing number from 0 to whatever the loop ends at. How can I accomplish this?

A: You can do this, but it would probably be easier to use the position of each image in the node-set:

```
<xsl:for-each select="hotel/images/image">
<a href="javascript:void(0);"
onClick="slideshow('slideshow.php?id=4110&count={posi
tion()}')" target="_blank">
<img src="{ThumbnailURL}" border="0"/>
</a>
</xsl:for-each>
```

Question 20: XML to XSLT

I'm transforming an XML file using XSLT, and defining some namespaces in my XSL file to allow the document to be transformed. Here's a cut-down version of the two files:

XML:

```
<?xml version="1.0" encoding="UTF-8"?>
<allGamesWeb creationDate="2005-06-08"
xmlns="allGamesWeb"
    xmlns:xsi="http://www.w3.org/2001/XMLSchema-
instance"
    xsi:schemaLocation="allGamesWeb http://games-
preview.real.com/rnfeedgamesdl/XMLSchemas/allGamesWeb
.xsd">

    <gameGroupList>
        <gameGroup priority="1"
title="Action/Adventure">
            <gameItem gameID="hamsterball"
gameType="web" priority="1"/>
            <gameItem gameID="insaniquariumdeluxe"
gameType="web" priority="2"/>
            <gameItem gameID="shroomz" gameType="web"
priority="3"/>
            <gameItem gameID="atomaders"
gameType="web" priority="1"/>
            <gameItem gameID="feedingfrenzy"
gameType="web" priority="2"/>
            <gameItem gameID="freakoutgold"
gameType="web" priority="3"/>
            <gameItem gameID="atomicpongling"
gameType="web" priority="4"/>
            <gameItem gameID="varmintz"
gameType="web" priority="5"/>
        </gameGroup>
    </gameGroupList>
</allGamesWeb>
```

XSL:

```
<?xml version='1.0'?>
<xsl:stylesheet
 xmlns:xsl="http://www.w3.org/1999/XSL/Transform"
 xmlns="http://www.w3.org/1999/xhtml"
 xmlns:game="game"
```

```
 xmlns:allGamesWeb="allGamesWeb"
 version="1.0">

  <xsl:output method="html"/>

  <xsl:template
match="/allGamesWeb:allGamesWeb/allGamesWeb:gameGroup
List">
  When using XSLT xmlns attribute added to output
html
    <xsl:for-each select="allGamesWeb:gameGroup">
        <p>
          <xsl:value-of
select="allGamesWeb:gameItem/@gameID" />
        </p>
    </xsl:for-each>

  </xsl:template>

</xsl:stylesheet>
```

Now when I combine the output it looks like this:

```
<p xmlns:allGamesWeb="allGamesWeb" xmlns:game="game"
xmlns="http://www.w3.org/1999/xhtml">hamsterball</p>
<p xmlns:allGamesWeb="allGamesWeb" xmlns:game="game"
xmlns="http://www.w3.org/1999/xhtml">insaniquariumdel
uxe</p>
<p xmlns:allGamesWeb="allGamesWeb" xmlns:game="game"
xmlns="http://www.w3.org/1999/xhtml">shroomz</p>
<p xmlns:allGamesWeb="allGamesWeb" xmlns:game="game"
xmlns="http://www.w3.org/1999/xhtml">atomaders</p>
<p xmlns:allGamesWeb="allGamesWeb" xmlns:game="game"
xmlns="http://www.w3.org/1999/xhtml">feedingfrenzy</p
>

<p xmlns:allGamesWeb="allGamesWeb" xmlns:game="game"
xmlns="http://www.w3.org/1999/xhtml">freakoutgold</p>
<p xmlns:allGamesWeb="allGamesWeb" xmlns:game="game"
xmlns="http://www.w3.org/1999/xhtml">atomicpongling</
p>
<p xmlns:allGamesWeb="allGamesWeb" xmlns:game="game"
xmlns="http://www.w3.org/1999/xhtml">varmintz</p>
```

As you can see, the XMLNS attributes of the XSL document are being added to the HTML elements of the output for some reason. Why is this happening? How do I stop it?

A: Use exclude-result-prefixes as an attribute for the xsl:stylesheet node, with a white space delimited list of values of namespaces you want to exclude from the output document (#default for default namespace):

```
exclude-result-prefixes="#default game allGamesWeb"
```

The XSL will add the namespaces by default to the top level element of the XML. Your output is not XML, because it's not well-formed. XML can only have one top level element. The parser is treating each element as a new XML document, thus, you need to add the namespaces to each one.

Question 21: Basic XSLT

I'm a complete beginner at XSLT. I'm still struggling to understand how to achieve a task. Take the following XML:

```
<DataHeader>
  <DataDetails>
    <F1>12345</F1>
    <F2>More Data</F2>
  </DataDetails>
</DataHeader>
```

I need to write an XSL document that converts it to this structure:

```
<?xml version="1.0" encoding="UTF-8"?>
<new>
  <cols>
    <col name="F1">12345</col>
    <col name="F2">More Data</col>
  </cols>
</new>
```

How can I do this right?

A: You can try this:

```
<?xml version="1.0"?>
<xsl:stylesheet version="1.0"
xmlns:xsl="http://www.w3.org/1999/XSL/Transform">
```

```
<xsl:output method = "xml" />

 <xsl:template match="/">
  <!-- always create elements new/cols -->
  <xsl:element name="new">
   <xsl:element name="cols">
    <!-- for each node in DataHeader/DataDetails ...
-->
    <xsl:for-each select =
"DataHeader/DataDetails/*">
     <!-- create an element with the name of current
node -->
     <xsl:element name="{name()}">
      <!-- and put the value of current node in -->
      <xsl:value-of select="."/>
     </xsl:element>
    </xsl:for-each>
   </xsl:element>
  </xsl:element>
 </xsl:template>
</xsl:stylesheet>
```

You don't need the element tags:

```
<?xml version="1.0" encoding="UTF-8"?>
<xsl:stylesheet version="1.0"
xmlns:xsl="http://www.w3.org/1999/XSL/Transform">
  <xsl:template match="/">
    <new>
      <cols>
        <xsl:for-each
select="DataHeader/DataDetails/*">
          <col name="{name(.)}">
            <xsl:value-of select="."/>
          </col>
        </xsl:for-each>
      </cols>
    </new>
  </xsl:template>
</xsl:stylesheet>
```

Question 22: Avoiding Repeating Values in an Option Box

I have the following XML:

```
<department>
<export>shoes</export>
<export>beds</export>
<export>blankets</export>
<export>cars</export>
<export>beds</export>
</department>
```

Using the above, is it possible to make a drop down menu of values in <export> and where a value is repeated, it would only appear as one? I want the following reflected:

drop down:
shoes
beds
blankets
cars

NOT:
shoes
beds
blankets
cars
beds

I have tried:

```
<xsl:template match="//document/">
              <xsl:variable
name="fred"></xsl:variable>
              <xsl:if test="not(fred='export')" >
            <option value="{export}"><xsl:value-of
select="export"/></option>
            </xsl:if>
           fred={export}
    </xsl:template>
```

How can I produce the results I want?

A: You can do this and check if the current node doesn't match a preceding node:

```
<xsl:template match="department">
  <xsl:for-each select="export">
    <xsl:sort select="."/>
    <xsl:if test="not(.=preceding::export)">
      <option value="{.}">
        <xsl:value-of select="."/>
      </option>
    </xsl:if>
  </xsl:for-each>
</xsl:template>
```

Question 23: Using CSS with XML/XSL

I've mastered HTML, CSS, PHP, and MySQL. I'm now trying XML/XSL. How would I use an external CSS style sheet with code generated by an XSL file? The examples that I've seen so far are a mixture of old fashioned HTML styling tags, in line styles, and tables.

Since I've gotten away from the HTML styling tags and tables, is it possible to just replace their functions with purely an XML/XSL codes?

A: It depends on what you are expecting XSL to do. It is generally used to transform XML into HTML. An example will generally look like this:

```
<?xml version="1.0" encoding="ISO-8859-1"?>
<xsl:stylesheet version="1.0"
xmlns:xsl="http://www.w3.org/1999/XSL/Transform">
  <xsl:template match="/">
  <html>
    <head>
      <link rel="stylesheet" type="text/css"
href="mycss.css" />
    </head>
    <body>
```

Below is another example if you want the CSS to be set by the XML:

```
<myxml>
  <mycss>mycss.css</mycss
  ...
</myxml>
```

You can do this:

```
<?xml version="1.0" encoding="ISO-8859-1"?>
<xsl:stylesheet version="1.0"
xmlns:xsl="http://www.w3.org/1999/XSL/Transform">
  <xsl:template match="/">
  <html>
    <head>
      <link rel="stylesheet" type="text/css"
href="{mycss}" />
    </head>
    <body>
```

If you want to use CSS without HTML tags, you can use it directly with XML so you won't need XSL. See this example: http://www.w3schools.com/xml/xml_display.asp.

Again, if you want to use XSL to arrive at the XML + CSS then look into this:
http://www.w3schools.com/xsl/el_processing-instruction.asp;

Such as:

```
<?xml version="1.0" encoding="ISO-8859-1"?>
<xsl:stylesheet version="1.0"
xmlns:xsl="http://www.w3.org/1999/XSL/Transform">
  <xsl:template match="/">
  <xsl:processing-instruction name="xml-stylesheet">
    href="<xsl:value-of select="mycss" />"
type="text/css"
  </xsl:processing-instruction>
  <article>
```

Question 24: Change Date Format in XSLT

How can I format my date as mm/dd/yyyy in XSLT? My SQL Server's date time field contains "5/3/2005 2:48:41 PM".

My XSLT code looks like this:

```
<xsl:value-of select="StartDate"/>
```

And my output looks s like this: "2005-05-03T14:48:41.0000000-04:00" which looks weird. How can I do it right?

A: If you intend to use XML explicitly within your SQL then it will be more efficient to just convert directly on the SQL server. See example below:

```
convert(varchar(10),dStartDate,103)
```

Or use:

```
<xsl:value-of
select="concat(substring(StartDate,6,2),'/',substring
(StartDate,9,2),'/',substring(StartDate,1,4))"/>
```

Question 25: XPath Axes in XSL

I need help with XPath Axes in XSL for any XML function. I need it so that the XSL is valid against any XML. I tried it with ancestor-or-self::* and similar things like it, but I think I don't really understand what it is all about.

For example, I want to visualize following XML with an XSL that is valid for any XML. My code looks like this:

```
<adressbuch>
<eintrag nr="1">
<name>Bernd Pack</name>
<adresse>Clausengasse 12</adresse>
<ort>1090 Wien</ort>
<email>bp@gmx.at</email>
<telefon>0650</telefon>
<geburtstag>12.12.1982</geburtstag>
</eintrag>
<eintrag nr="2">
<name>Patricia Bauer</name>
<adresse>Pflanzsteig 16</adresse>
<ort>1090 Wien</ort>
<email>pb@aon.at</email>
<telefon>06602</telefon>
<geburtstag>01.03.1957</geburtstag>
</eintrag>
</adressbuch>
```

So now I need an XSL which visualizes my XML above (and any other XML). For example, every "eintrag" should be visualized with number1.jpg and any child -> "name" til "geburtstag" shall be visualized with number2.jpg. How can I do that?

I tried the following XSL which does not really work:

```
<xsl:template match="/">
<xsl:element name="root">
<xsl:call-template name="visual"/>
</xsl:element>
</xsl:template>
<xsl:template name="visual">
<xsl:for-each select="//*">
<xsl:sort select="ancestor-or-self::*"
order="descending"/>
<xsl:if test="position()=1">
```

```
<xsl:value-of select="ancestor-or-self::*"/>
</xsl:if>
</xsl:for-each>
</xsl:template>
```

A: To reiterate, you're saying given a structure like this below:

```
<root>
  <node1>
    <node2>one</node2>
    <node2>two></node2>
  </node1>
</root>
```

You want something like:

```
<html>
  <head>
    <title>Visual XML</title>
  </head>
  <body>
    <img src="number1.jpg" alt="XML, node depth 1" />
    <img src="number2.jpg" alt="XML, node depth 2" />
    <img src="number2.jpg" alt="XML, node depth 2" />
  </body>
</html>
```

In which case you could use recursion:

```
<?xml version="1.0" encoding="UTF-8"?>
<xsl:stylesheet version="1.0"
xmlns:xsl="http://www.w3.org/1999/XSL/Transform">
  <xsl:template match="/">
    <html>
      <head>
        <title>Visual XML</title>
      </head>
      <body>
        <xsl:for-each select="*/*">
          <xsl:call-template name="visualize">
            <xsl:with-param name="node" select="."/>
            <xsl:with-param name="depth" select="1"/>
          </xsl:call-template>
        </xsl:for-each>
      </body>
    </html>
  </xsl:template>
```

```
  <xsl:template name="visualize">
    <xsl:param name="node"/>
    <xsl:param name="depth"/>
    <img src="number{$depth}.jpg" alt="XML, node
depth {$depth}"/>
    <xsl:if test="$node/*">
      <xsl:for-each select="$node/*">
        <xsl:call-template name="visualize">
          <xsl:with-param name="node" select="."/>
          <xsl:with-param name="depth"
select="$depth+1"/>
        </xsl:call-template>
      </xsl:for-each>
    </xsl:if>
  </xsl:template>
</xsl:stylesheet>
```

Question 26: Day from Month Function

I am trying to strip the day, month, and year as separate fields in XSLT using the following function:

```
 <CreationDateTimeDay><month-from-date(xs:date("2005-
04-23"))/></CreationDateTimeDay>
```

However, it's not working. What changes do I need to do to make it work?

A: You can try the following:

```
<CreationDateTimeDay><xsl:value-of select="month-
from-date(xs:date('2005-04-
23'))"/></CreationDateTimeDay>
```

Remember that this is an XPath 2 function.

Question 27: XSL Processor

Is the XSLT 1.0 processor like the Saxson XSLT processor necessary to view an XSL output? Or can you view the corresponding XSL output some other way?

A: An XSLT processor of some sort is always necessary. Internet Explorer (v5 and above I think) has MSXSL built in. See: http://www.w3schools.com/xsl/xsl_browsers.asp. So all you need to do is create an XML file and an XSL file, then reference the XSL file in the XML file, then opens the XML file in IE. See: http://www.w3schools.com/xsl/xsl_transformation.asp.

Question 28: XSL: for-each and not()

I am trying to do a for-each, but I want to leave out certain nodes. It should go something like this:

```
<xsl:for-each select="/Report/*[not(/Totals)]">
```

In other words, I want all the nodes under Report, except the "Totals" nodes. Is this possible?

A: Try the following codes:

```
<xsl:for-each select="/Report/*[local-name() !=
'Totals']">
```

The above codes might do it. Your method would work too, with some changes:

```
<xsl:for-each select="/Report/*[not(Totals)]">
```

Rather than /Totals. You simply needed:

```
Select="/Report/PageLevel"
```

Since there are no other nodes under Report besides Page Level and Totals.

Question 29: XSLT <xsl:text> no Whitespace Output

Is there any way to tell the <xsl:text> directive not to output any white space. I tried to generate an HTML <img> tag for the purpose as shown below:

When I use:

```
<xsl:text disable-output-escaping="yes">
  &lt;img src="
</xsl:text>

  <xsl:value-of select="."/>

<xsl:text disable-output-escaping="yes">
  "/&gt;
</xsl:text>
```

The output is:

```
<img src="
    file://C:\java\xslt\px_logo.gif
    "/>
```

And in order to have it appear on one line, I use this:

```
<xsl:text disable-output-escaping="yes">
    &lt;img src="</xsl:text><xsl:value-of
select="."/><xsl:text disable-output-
escaping="yes">"/&gt;
    </xsl:text>
```

It produces the desired output, but this is not very readable. Is there a better way?

A: You can try this instead:

```
<img src="{.}" />
```

Question 30: Conditional Variables

I have this form that shows contents and makes calculations based on the XML content, via an XSL document. I set up the variables to handle the calculations. The basic calculations were something this:

```
$Material = "QTY * MatlCost * MatlLength"
$Spring   = "QTY * SprgCost * SprgQTY"
$Adapter  = "QTY * AdptCost * AdptQTY"
$Machine  = "QTY * MachCost * (MachIDLen +
MachODLen)"
$Total    = "$Material + $Spring + $Adapter +
$Machine"
```

Now the problem is, if there was no adapter, the AdptCost & AdptQTY would return NaN (Not a Number) which would cause the $Adapter to return NaN, which would in turn cause the $Total to return NaN. I needed a way to set the variable to 0 if the Element did not exist. The way I was displaying the line items was such as this:

```
<tr>
  <td>Description</td>
  <td>QTY</td>
  <td>Rate</td>
  <td>Length</td>
  <td>Total</td>
</tr>
<xsl:if test="MatlCost">
  <tr>
    <td>Material</td>
    <td><xsl:value-of select="QTY" /></td>
    <td><xsl:value-of select="MatlCost" /></td>
    <td><xsl:value-of select="MatlLength" /></td>
    <td><xsl:value-of select="$Material" /></td>
  </tr>
</xsl:if>
<xsl:if test="SprgCost">
  <tr>
    <td>Spring</td>
    <td><xsl:value-of select="QTY * SprgQTY" /></td>
    <td><xsl:value-of select="SprgCost" /></td>
    <td></td>
    <td><xsl:value-of select="$Spring" /></td>
  </tr>
</xsl:if>
```

```
<xsl:if test="AdptCost">
  <tr>
    <td>Adapter</td>
    <td><xsl:value-of select="QTY * AdptQTY" /></td>
    <td><xsl:value-of select="AdptCost" /></td>
    <td></td>
    <td><xsl:value-of select="$Adapter" /></td>
  </tr>
</xsl:if>
<xsl:if test="MachCost">
  <tr>
    <td>Adapter</td>
    <td><xsl:value-of select="QTY" /></td>
    <td><xsl:value-of select="MachCost" /></td>
    <td><xsl:value-of select="MachIDLen + MachODLen"
/></td>
    <td><xsl:value-of select="$Machine" /></td>
  </tr>
</xsl:if>
<tr>
  <td colspan="4">Grand Total</td>
  <td><xsl:value-of select="$Total" /></td>
</tr>
```

So I tried this at first:

```
<xsl:if test="AdptCost">
  <xsl:variable name="Adapter" select="QTY * AdptCost
* AdptQTY" />
</xsl:if>
<xsl:if test="not(AdptCost)">
  <xsl:variable name="Adapter" select="0" />
</xsl:if>
```

Which did not work. I then tried <xsl:choose> as well. But it turns out that if you define the variable in an IF or CHOOSE block, it is limited to the scope within the block you defined it in. How else can I assign variables effectively?

A: There are two ways to assign variables. One is as shown below:

```
<xsl:variable name="Adapter" select="X" />
```

Or:

```
<xsl:variable name="Adapter">
  <xsl:value-of select="X" />
</xsl:variable>
```

You can also invert it, and try this:

```
<xsl:variable name="Adapter">
  <xsl:if test="AdptCost">
    <xsl:value-of select="QTY * AdptCost * AdptQTY">
  </xsl:if>
  <xsl:if test="not(AdptCost)">
    <xsl:value-of select="0">
  </xsl:if>
</xsl:variable>
```

This is how conditional variables are created. There are multiple uses for them so can get creative. You can use <xsl:choose> in place of the <xsl:if> blocks with this if you have multiple conditions. You could also combine this with a call template, to shorten the code in some cases, especially if there are multiple variables, with common patterns.

Question 31: Counting Number the of Characters

I want to accomplish the following. If the paragraph is the second one, and it has less than 200 characters, then I want to display the next one. Here is what I have:

```
 <xsl:if test="count(preceding-sibling::p) = 2">
        <p>
        <xsl:apply-templates />
      </p>
     </xsl:if>
```

How do I add the condition for the preceding paragraph to have less than 200 characters? What would that condition look like?

A: You can try using the string-length function like this:

```
"string-length(preceding-sibling::p) &lt; 200"
```

You'll need to put “to” and "and" with the statement if you can.

Question 32: Showing hashdata on HTML Table with XSL

Is it possible to show the following structure (made with XML::Dumper in Perl) in the HTML table with XSL, so that item under arrayref would be its own row in the HTML table?

```
<!DOCTYPE xml>
<?xml-stylesheet href="test.xsl" type="text/xsl"?>
<perldata>
 <hashref>
  <item key="res">
   <arrayref memory_address="0x1d85438">
    <item key="0">1</item>
    <item key="1">2</item>
    <item key="2">3</item>
   </arrayref>
  </item>
  <item key="res2">
   <arrayref memory_address="0x1d85439">
    <item key="0">1</item>
    <item key="1">2</item>
    <item key="2">3</item>
   </arrayref>
  </item>
 </hashref>
</perldata>
```

I tried this, but it doesn't work correctly. How do I apply template4 for item, when arrayref template is run?

```
<?xml version="1.0" encoding="ISO-8859-1" ?>
<xsl:stylesheet version="1.0"
xmlns:xsl="http://www.w3.org/1999/XSL/Transform">
  <xsl:output method="html" version="1.0"
encoding="iso-8859-1" indent="yes"/>
  <xsl:template match="/">
    <xsl:apply-templates />
  </xsl:template>

  <xsl:template match="perldata">
    <xsl:apply-templates />
  </xsl:template>
```

```
  <xsl:template match="hashref">
    <table border="1">
      <xsl:apply-templates />
    </table>
  </xsl:template>

   <xsl:template match="arrayref">
     <tr>
       <td>
          <xsl:apply-templates />
       </td>
    </tr>
  </xsl:template>

  <xsl:template match="item">
    <td>
      <xsl:copy-of select="." />
    </td>
  </xsl:template>

</xsl:stylesheet>
```

A: You've got nodes named <item> on two levels:

```
childnode of <hashref>, and childnodes of <arrayref>.
```

When your style sheet says:

```
<xsl:template match="hashref">
  <table border="1">
    <xsl:apply-templates />
  </table>
</xsl:template>
the nodes below <hashref> (which are <item>-nodes are
parsed with:
<xsl:template match="item">
  <td>
    <xsl:copy-of select="." />
  </td>
</xsl:template>
```

The above code is probably not what you had in mind. This would be a simple way to fix that:

```
<xsl:template match="hashref/item">
  <table border="1">
    <xsl:apply-templates />
```

```
  </table>
</xsl:template>
```

Also, code: “<xsl:copy-of select=".">” copies the whole node into your output. Usually you wouldn’t want <td><item key="0">1</item></td> in your HTML. If you use <xsl:value-of select=".">, you get <td>1</td>;

Question 33: XSL for an Attribute

I am trying to make an “if statement” in my XSL for this XML doc, it only needs to show the value of a content when the typeid = 2:

```
<xml>
<contents>
<content typeid="1">aaaaa</content>
<content typeid="1">aaaaa</content>
<content typeid="1">aaaaa</content>
<content typeid="2">bbbbb</content>
<content typeid="1">aaaaa</content>
</contents>
</xml>
```

This is the code I am trying to use:

```
<xsl:for-each select=/xml/contents/content">
<xsl:value-of select="@typeid"/>
   <xsl:if test="string=2">
        <xsl:value-of select="@typeid"/>
   </xsl:if>
</xsl:for-each>
```

How can I resolve this?

A: You can do the following:

```
<xsl:for-each
select=/xml/contents/content[@typeid=2]">
  <!-- only nodes with typeid = 2 -->
  <xsl:value-of select="."/>
</xsl:for-each>
```

Or:

```
<xsl:for-each select=/xml/contents/content">
<!-- all content-nodes -->
  <xsl:if test="@typeid=2">
  <!-- only nodes with typeid = 2 -->
    <xsl:value-of select="."/>
  </xsl:if>
</xsl:for-each>
```

If you want better performance without any looping through each node, use the code below:

```
<xsl:value-of
select="/xml/contents/content[@typeid=1][3]"/>
```

Question 34: XSL Question

I want to turn an XML document into a form page. How can I apply a default value to a text input field? Here's how I would do this in HTML:

```
<input type="text" value="My Default Value">
```

When displayed in a browser, a text input field would appear with "My Default Value" as the default value. I can create a text input field with my xsl style sheet like this below:

```
<td><INPUT TYPE="text"/></td>
```

However I run into problems trying to set the "value" with <xsl:value-of select="XML_TAG_CONTAINING_DEFAULT_DATA"/> as this is meaningless within the HTML tag.

Is there some sort of escape mechanism (escape character) to assign such a value within the HTML tag? Is there any way to do this?

A: You'll find things a little more robust if you build your HTML using a combination of the <xsl:element> and <xsl:attribute> tags.

```
<xsl:element name="input">
 <xsl:attribute name="type">text</xsl:attribute>
 <xsl:attribute name="value">
  <xsl:value-of
select="XML_TAG_CONTAINING_DEFAULT_DATA" />
 </xsl:attribute>
</xsl:element>
```

Question 35: XSLT Resources

What resources can I possibly use that would lead me to the answer to the following question? I have an XML file which I control so I can add attributes when necessary:

```
<page id="1" parent=0">
<page id="2" parent=0">
<page id="3" parent=2">
<page id="4" parent=2">
<page id="5" parent=4">
<page id="6" parent=4">
<page id="7" parent=4">
<page id="8" parent=2">
<page id="9" parent=2">
<page id="10" parent=0">
<page id="11" parent=0">
<page id="12" parent=11">
<page id="13" parent=11">
<page id="14" parent=0">
<page id="15" parent=0">
```

Thus, and example of the full structure indicated above would be:

```
1
2
    3
    4
        5
        6
        7
    8
    9
10
11
    12
```

```
    13
14
15
```

But I need to offer up to three levels where the page ID will drive the transformation. I can certainly access the page ID and am assuming I can use a parameter in the XLST such that:

=> where page ID = 6

```
1
2
    3
    4
        5
        *6
        7
10
11
14
15
```

=> where page ID = 12

```
1
2
10
11
    *12
    13
14
15
```

=> where page ID = 2

```
*1
2
10
11
14
15
```

A: It would be easier if the XML is already nested.

```
<root>
   <page id="1" parent="0">ONE</page>
```

```
    <page id="2" parent="0">TWO</page>
    <page id="3" parent="2">THREE</page>
    <page id="4" parent="2">FOUR</page>
    <page id="5" parent="4">FIVE</page>
    <page id="6" parent="4">SIX</page>
    <page id="7" parent="4">SEVEN</page>
    <page id="8" parent="2">EIGHT</page>
    <page id="9" parent="2">NINE</page>
    <page id="10" parent="0">TEN</page>
    <page id="11" parent="0">ELEVEN</page>
    <page id="12" parent="11">TWELVE</page>
    <page id="13" parent="11">THIRTEEN</page>
    <page id="14" parent="0">FOURTEEN</page>
    <page id="15" parent="0">FIFTEEN</page>
</root>


<?xml version="1.0"?>
<xsl:stylesheet version="1.0"
xmlns:xsl="http://www.w3.org/1999/XSL/Transform">
    <xsl:output method="html" encoding="Windows-1252"
/>
    <xsl:variable name="pageId" select="6" />

    <xsl:template match="/">
        <html>
            <head>
            </head>

            <body>
                <xsl:call-template name="makeLevel">
                    <xsl:with-param name="selectedPage"
select="//page[@id=$pageId]" />
                </xsl:call-template>
            </body>
        </html>
    </xsl:template>

    <xsl:template name="makeLevel">
        <xsl:param name="selectedPage" />
        <xsl:param name="insert" />

        <xsl:choose>
            <xsl:when test="$selectedPage">
                <xsl:call-template name="makeLevel">
                    <xsl:with-param name="selectedPage"
select="//page[@id=$selectedPage/@parent]" />
```

```
                <xsl:with-param name="insert">
                   <table border="1">
                      <xsl:for-each
select="//page[@parent=$selectedPage/@parent]">
                         <tr>
                            <td>
                               <xsl:if test="@id =
$pageId">*</xsl:if>

                               <xsl:value-of
select="." />
                            </td>
                         </tr>
                         <xsl:if
test="@id=$selectedPage/@id and $insert">
                            <tr>
                               <td width="10">
                               </td>
                               <td>
                                  <xsl:copy-of
select="$insert" />
                               </td>
                            </tr>
                         </xsl:if>
                      </xsl:for-each>
                   </table>
                </xsl:with-param>
             </xsl:call-template>
          </xsl:when>

          <xsl:otherwise>
             <xsl:copy-of select="$insert" />
          </xsl:otherwise>
       </xsl:choose>
    </xsl:template>
</xsl:stylesheet>
```

Question 36: Sorting in XSL

I need to sort the libraries in each county by LIBRARY_NAME. Where do I place the following XSL file?

```
<xsl:sort select="LIBRARY_NAME"/>
```

Below are samples of short versions of each file:

```
 <LIBRARIES>
 <COUNTY>
  <COUNTY_NAME>Boone</COUNTY_NAME>

  <LIBRARY>
   <LIBRARY_NAME>Lebanon Public
Library</LIBRARY_NAME>
    <ADDRESS>104 E Washington St.</ADDRESS>
    <CITY>Lebanon</CITY>
    <STATE>IN</STATE>
    <ZIP>46052</ZIP>
    <PHONE>(765) 482-3460</PHONE>
    <FAX>(317) 873-5059 </FAX>
    <WEB>www.bccn.boone.in.us/LPL/index.html</WEB>
   </LIBRARY>

  <LIBRARY>
   <LIBRARY_NAME>Thorntown Public
Library</LIBRARY_NAME>
    <ADDRESS>124 N. Market St.</ADDRESS>
    <CITY>Thorntown</CITY>
    <STATE>IN</STATE>
    <ZIP>46071</ZIP>
    <PHONE>(765) 436-7348</PHONE>
    <FAX>(765) 436-7011</FAX>
    <WEB>www.bccn.boone.in.us/tpl</WEB>
  </LIBRARY>
  <LIBRARY>
    <LIBRARY_NAME>Hussey-Mayfield Memorial Public
Library</LIBRARY_NAME>
    <ADDRESS>250 N. 5th St.</ADDRESS>
    <CITY>Zionsville</CITY>
    <STATE>IN</STATE>
    <ZIP>46077</ZIP>
    <PHONE>(317) 873-3149</PHONE>
    <FAX>(317) 873-8339</FAX>
    <WEB>www.zionsville.lib.in.us</WEB>
   </LIBRARY>
```

```
 </COUNTY>
</LIBRARIES>
```

Here is My XSL:

```
<xsl:output method="html" indent="yes"/>

<xsl:template match="/">                    <!--root
rule-->
  <html>
    <head><title>County Libraries</title></head>
    <body><xsl:apply-templates/>
    </body>
  </html>
</xsl:template>

<xsl:template match="COUNTY">
  <xsl:apply-templates select="COUNTY_NAME"/>
  <xsl:apply-templates select="LIBRARY"/>
</xsl:template>

<xsl:template match="COUNTY/COUNTY_NAME">  <!-- Get
the name of the county and display in in a table
cell-->
  <table width="80%">
  <tr>
  <td bgcolor="#99ccff"> <!--When you spit out the
HTML, add an a name link for each county name, thus
creating a link for the clickable map-->
<h3><a><xsl:attribute name="name"><xsl:apply-
templates/></xsl:attribute></a><xsl:apply-templates/>
<xsl:text> County</xsl:text></h3>
  </td>
  </tr>
  </table>
</xsl:template>

<xsl:template match="LIBRARY"><!-- get each library
for the county and display it-->
<b><xsl:apply-templates
select="LIBRARY_NAME"/></b><br/>
<xsl:apply-templates select="ADDRESS"/><br/>
  <xsl:apply-templates select="CITY"/><xsl:text>,
</xsl:text>
  <xsl:apply-templates select="STATE"/><xsl:text>
</xsl:text>
  <xsl:apply-templates select="ZIP"/><br/>
```

```
  <xsl:text>Phone: </xsl:text><xsl:apply-templates
select="PHONE"/><br/>
  <xsl:text>FAX: </xsl:text><xsl:apply-templates
select="FAX"/><br/>
  <xsl:text>WEB: </xsl:text>
  <a><xsl:attribute name="href"> <!--make the web
address a hot link-->
    <xsl:text>http://</xsl:text><xsl:apply-templates
select="WEB"/>
    </xsl:attribute>
    <i><xsl:value-of select="WEB"/></i>
    </a>
    <p> </p>
</xsl:template>

</xsl:stylesheet>
```

A: This should work for your needs:

```
<xsl:template match="COUNTY">
  <xsl:apply-templates select="COUNTY_NAME">
      <xsl:sort select="COUNTY_NAME"/>
  </xsl:apply-templates>
  <xsl:apply-templates select="LIBRARY">
      <xsl:sort select="LIBRARY_NAME"/>
  </xsl:apply-templates>
</xsl:template>
```

You can also make a slight modification, so that the counties would sort when not in order on the XML file. Make a separate template match.

```
<xsl:template match="LIBRARIES">  <!--when you get
the counties, sort them in alpha order-->
  <xsl:apply-templates select="COUNTY">
      <xsl:sort select="COUNTY_NAME"
order="ascending"/>
  </xsl:apply-templates>
</xsl:template>

<xsl:template match="COUNTY"> <!--when you get the
libraries in a county, sort them in alpha order-->
  <xsl:apply-templates select="COUNTY_NAME">
  </xsl:apply-templates>
  <xsl:apply-templates select="LIBRARY">
      <xsl:sort select="LIBRARY_NAME"/>
  </xsl:apply-templates>
</xsl:template>
```

Question 37: Transform .XSD Files to a XML File

I have several schema files; one schema file includes several other schema files. For example:

```
<xs:include schemaLocation="C:\myCodes.xsd"/>.
```

I would like to transform the schema files into an XML file. How can I use XSLT to get the nodes and attributes which are in the included files? I have tried to use:

```
<xsl:foreach
select="document(myCodes.xsd)\xs:complexType")
```

But I could not get it work.

A: If you have to use imports like these, always stuff them in threads in case you want to pull more data out of the file later in different XPath statements. That way you don't have to do the document statement over and over. I have simple XML file, XSD file, and XSL file examples. The XML is from my JFaceDBc plugin for eclipse.

```
<Beans>
    <Bean
Class="net.sourceforge.squirrel_sql.fw.sql.SQLAlias">
        <activate>false</activate>
        <driverIdentifier
Class="net.sourceforge.squirrel_sql.fw.id.UidIdentifi
er">
            <string>-4</string>
        </driverIdentifier>
        <identifier
Class="net.sourceforge.squirrel_sql.fw.id.UidIdentifi
er">
            <string>aasdf</string>
        </identifier>
        <name>asdf</name>
        <password>asdf</password>
        <url>asdf</url>
        <userName>asdf</userName>
    </Bean>
</Beans>
```

```
<xs:schema
xmlns:xs="http://www.w3.org/2001/XMLSchema">
<xs:element name="selfTest">
<xs:annotation>
<xs:documentation>Comment describing your root
element</xs:documentation>
</xs:annotation>
</xs:element>
</xs:schema>
```

```
<?xml version="1.0" encoding="UTF-8"?>
<xsl:stylesheet version="1.0"
xmlns:xsl="http://www.w3.org/1999/XSL/Transform"
xmlns:xs="http://www.w3.org/2001/XMLSchema">
    <xsl:variable name="schema"
select="document('selfTest.xsd')"/>
    <xsl:template match="/">
        <Beans>
            <xsl:for-each select="Beans/Bean">
                <xsl:sort select="name"/>
                <xsl:copy-of select="."/>
            </xsl:for-each>
            <xsl:value-of
select="$schema/xs:schema/xs:element/xs:annotation/xs
:documentation"/>
        </Beans>
    </xsl:template>
</xsl:stylesheet>
```

Question 38: XSLT - Recompose Simple XML

I've got an XML storing all products on the same level on a flat structure. A few products belong to other products. How can I recompose my XML to fit my situation? How can I move the products underneath their parent-product? I do have a prodID for each product and a parentProdID. For example:

```
<prod>
   <prodName>Wheel</prodName>
   <prodID>1234</prodName>
   <parentProdID>23</parentProdID>
</prod
```

A: Try this one. It's not too hard to figure out how it works.

```
<?xml version="1.0"?>
<xsl:stylesheet version="1.0"
xmlns:xsl="http://www.w3.org/1999/XSL/Transform">
   <xsl:output method="xml" />

   <xsl:template match="/">
      <xsl:apply-templates select="//prod[not
(parentProdID &gt; 0)]" />
   </xsl:template>

   <xsl:template match="prod">
      <xsl:element name="prod">
         <xsl:variable name="id" select="prodID" />
         <xsl:apply-templates />
         <xsl:apply-templates
select="../prod[parentProdID=$id]" />
      </xsl:element>
   </xsl:template>

   <xsl:template match="prod/*">
      <xsl:copy-of select="." />
   </xsl:template>

</xsl:stylesheet>
```

Question 39: XSL:value of Select Attribute

I am not very experienced in XML. There is an XML style sheet using this format:

```
<xsl:for-each select="depthem">
 Depth Encoding Method: <xsl:value-of/>
</xsl:for-each>
```

It seems that a select attribute is required in xsl:value-of, but I'm not sure what to use to replace it with. Here's what I have:

```
<xsl:for-each select="depthem">
 Depth Encoding Method: <xsl:value-of/>
</xsl:for-each>
```

What should I use?

A: The xsl:for-each lets you loop through a series of repeated elements. So if depthem occurs multiple times in the context node, you will loop over each element. If you are looking to print the value of either a child, an attribute, or a text, then you use the <xsl:value-of select=""/> to display that value.

```
<!-- Select the current nodes text -->
<xsl:value-of select="."/> or <xsl:value-of
select="text()"/>

<!-- Select the current nodes attribute -->
<xsl:value-of select="@ATTRIBUTE_NAME"/>

<!-- Select the current nodes child -->
<xsl:value-of select="CHILD_NAME"/>
```

Question 40: Transform Some XML Data Using XSL

I am trying to transform some XML data using XSL. I have a bunch of invoices encoded in XML and I want to display them all in a browser. I need to convert an XSL sheet that is geared to display one invoice (with a slightly different data set) to display many invoices. Here is an abbreviated version of the XML:

```
<?xml version="1.0" encoding="UTF-8" ?>
<?xml-stylesheet href="invoice.xsl" type="text/xsl"?>
<database URL="jdbc:odbc:flamingo">
    <invoices QUERY="SELECT * FROM invoice WHERE
shipToState = 'NSW'">
        <invoices_rec>
            <invoiceNum>102</invoiceNum>
            <salesDate>30. Jul. 01</salesDate>
            <shipToAddress>11 Hollsworth
St</shipToAddress>
            <shipToCity>Paramatta</shipToCity>
            <shipToState>NSW</shipToState>
            <shipToZip>2421</shipToZip>
            <contactName>Sally</contactName>
            <contactPhone>6789-4321</contactPhone>
        </invoices_rec>
    </invoices>
    <lines QUERY="SELECT i.invoiceNum, l.prodCode,
l.salesQty, p.prodName, p.prodDesc,
p.prodPrice, l.salesQty * p.prodPrice AS
extendedPrice FROM invoice i INNER JOIN
(lines l INNER JOIN products p ON l.prodCode =
p.prodCode) ON
i.invoiceNum = l.invoiceNum WHERE i.shipToState =
'NSW'">
        <lines_rec>
            <invoiceNum>102</invoiceNum>
            <prodCode>FP002</prodCode>
            <salesQty>20</salesQty>
            <prodName>Flamingo Towels</prodName>
            <prodDesc>Terry towling material printed
with flamingos</prodDesc>
            <prodPrice>$15.00</prodPrice>
            <extendedPrice>$300.00</extendedPrice>
        </lines_rec>
        <lines_rec>
            <invoiceNum>103</invoiceNum>
            <prodCode>FP002</prodCode>
```

```
            <salesQty>10</salesQty>
            <prodName>Flamingo Towels</prodName>
            <prodDesc>Terry towling material printed
with flamingos</prodDesc>
            <prodPrice>$15.00</prodPrice>
            <extendedPrice>$150.00</extendedPrice>
        </lines_rec>
    </lines>
    <bottom QUERY="SELECT i.invoiceNum,
Sum(l.salesQty * p.prodPrice) AS subtotal FROM
invoice i
INNER JOIN (lines l INNER JOIN products p ON
l.prodCode = p.prodCode) ON
i.invoiceNum = l.invoiceNum
GROUP BY i.invoiceNum">
        <bottom_rec>
            <invoiceNum>102</invoiceNum>
            <subtotal>$2,459.00</subtotal>
        </bottom_rec>
        <bottom_rec>
            <invoiceNum>103</invoiceNum>
            <subtotal>$2,026.00</subtotal>
        </bottom_rec>
    </bottom>
</database>
```

Here is the XSL style sheet with which I am working on:

```
<?xml version="1.0"?>
<xsl:stylesheet version="1.0"
xmlns:xsl="http://www.w3.org/1999/XSL/Transform">

<xsl:output method="html" indent="yes"/>
<!-- Main rule -->
<xsl:template match="/">
  <html>
   <head>
    <title>
      Invoice
    </title>
  </head>
  <body bgcolor="#FFFFFF">

<H2 align="right"><font
color="blue">INVOICE</font></H2>
   <table cellpadding="5" width="100%">
     <tr valign="top">
        <td width="15%">
```

```
      <font color="blue">Ship To:</font>
    </td>
    <td width="35%">
    <font size="-1">
          <xsl:apply-templates
select="*/*/invoices_rec"/>
    </font>
    </td>
        <td width="15%">
      <font color="blue">Bill To:</font>
    </td>
    <td width="35%">
    <font size="-1">
          <xsl:apply-templates
select="*/*/billTo_rec"/>
    </font>
    </td>
     </tr>
   </table>
   <p/>
   <table border="1" bordercolor="blue" width="100%">

     <tr bgcolor="blue">
    <xsl:apply-templates select="*/orderec"/>
     </tr>
     <tr>
    <xsl:apply-templates select="*/*/orderec_rec"/>
     </tr>
    </table>
   <p/>
   <table border="0" cellpadding="2" width="100%">
      <xsl:apply-templates
select="*/products[position()=1]"/>
      <xsl:apply-templates
select='/database/products/products_rec'/>
   </table>
<hr size="3"/>
<div align="right">
  <table width="40%">
   <xsl:for-each select="*/buttom/*/*">
    <tr>
      <td>
       <font color="blue"><xsl:value-of
select="@NAME"/>:</font>
     </td>
     <td align="right">
      <xsl:apply-templates/>
     </td>
    </tr>
```

```
    </xsl:for-each>
  </table>
  </div>

  </body>
  </html>
</xsl:template>

<!-- Left header  -->
<xsl:template match="invoices_rec">
    <xsl:for-each select="./*">
    <xsl:apply-templates/>
    <br/>
    </xsl:for-each>
</xsl:template>

<!-- Right header  -->
<xsl:template match="shipTo_rec">
    <xsl:for-each select="./*">
    <xsl:apply-templates/>
    <br/>
    </xsl:for-each>
</xsl:template>

<!-- Main body for order  -->
<xsl:template match="orderec_rec">
    <xsl:for-each select="./*">
      <td align="center">
    <font color="black" size="-1">
         <xsl:if test="@ISNULL">
            
         </xsl:if>
         <xsl:apply-templates/>
    </font>
      </td>
    </xsl:for-each>
</xsl:template>

<!-- Main header for order  -->
<xsl:template match="orderec">
    <xsl:for-each select="./*/*">
    <td align="center">
      <font color="white" size="-1">
         <xsl:value-of select="@NAME"/>:
      </font>
    </td>
    </xsl:for-each>
</xsl:template>
```

```
<!-- Main Table -->
<xsl:template match="products">
  <xsl:for-each select="./*[position()=1]">
   <!-- Main Table header -->
     <tr bgcolor="blue">
    <xsl:for-each select="./*">
     <td align="center">
       <font color="white" size="-1">
     <xsl:value-of select="@NAME"/>:
       </font>
      </td>
    </xsl:for-each>
    </tr>
  </xsl:for-each>
</xsl:template>

<xsl:template match="products_rec">
   <tr>
    <xsl:for-each select="./*">
      <td align="left">
    <font color="black" size="-1">
         <xsl:if test="@ISNULL">
            
         </xsl:if>
         <xsl:apply-templates/>
    </font>
      </td>
    </xsl:for-each>
   </tr>
</xsl:template>

</xsl:stylesheet>
```

Again, the XSL sheet is not written for the exact same data set, but should require some minor tweaking. When using a <xsl:for-each select="/*/*/invoice_rec> right after the <body> tag, instead of displaying multiple invoices nothing is displayed.

How do I fix this?

A: I had a look at your XSL, but it doesn't make sense: it refers to nodes (billTo_rec) and attributes (@NAME) that doesn't exist in your xml-source. But, as an example, here's an idea on how to approach it: Put the 'primary key' in a variable, and use it in x-path expressions to 'filter' the records in other 'tables'.

```
<?xml version="1.0"?>
<xsl:stylesheet version="1.0"
xmlns:xsl="http://www.w3.org/1999/XSL/Transform">
   <xsl:output method="html" indent="yes" />

   <xsl:template match="/">
      <html>
         <head>
            <title>Invoice</title>
         </head>

         <body bgcolor="#FFFFFF">
            <H2 align="right">
               <font color="blue">INVOICE</font>
            </H2>

            <xsl:for-each select="//invoices_rec">
                <xsl:variable name ="invoicenum"
select="invoiceNum"/>
                 <table cellpadding="5" width="100%">
                   <tr valign="top">
                      <td width="15%">
                         <font color="blue">Ship
To:</font>
                      </td>
                      <td width="35%">
                         <font size="-1">
                            <xsl:call-template
name="DisplayFields"/>
                         </font>
                      </td>
                      <td width="15%">
                         <font color="blue">Bill
To:</font>
                      </td>
                      <td width="35%">
                         <font size="-1">
                            <xsl:text>Don't know what
to display</xsl:text>
                         </font>
                      </td>
                   </tr>
                </table>
                <p />
                <table border="1" bordercolor="blue"
width="100%">
                      <xsl:apply-templates
select="//lines_rec[invoiceNum=$invoicenum]" />
                </table>
```

```
                <p />
                <table width="40%">
                   <xsl:apply-templates
select="//bottom_rec[invoiceNum=$invoicenum]" />
                  </table>
            </xsl:for-each>
         </body>
      </html>
   </xsl:template>


    <xsl:template name ="DisplayFields">
    <!-- as I don't know what labels to display, just
take the nodename -->
        <xsl:for-each select="*[position()!=1]">
            <xsl:value-of select= "name()"/>
            <xsl:text>: </xsl:text>
            <xsl:value-of select= "."/>
            <br/>
        </xsl:for-each>
    </xsl:template>

    <xsl:template match="lines_rec">
        <xsl:if test="position()=1">
            <tr bgcolor="blue">
                <xsl:for-each
select="*[position()!=1]">
                    <td align="center">
                        <font color="white"
size="-1">
                            <xsl:value-of
select="name()"/>
                        </font>
                    </td>
                </xsl:for-each>
            </tr>
        </xsl:if>
        <tr>
            <xsl:for-each select="*[position()!=1]">
                <td align="center">
                    <font color="black" size="-1">
                        <xsl:value-of select="."/>
                    </font>
                </td>
            </xsl:for-each>
        </tr>
    </xsl:template>

    <xsl:template match="bottom_rec">
```

```
        <tr>
            <td>subtotal</td>
            <td>
                <xsl:value-of select = "subtotal"/>
            </td>
        </tr>
    </xsl:template>

</xsl:stylesheet>
```

Now, if you want to modify the DisplayFields template so that not all nodes were displayed, except the address fields, you could say: "parse all nodes, except..."

```
    <xsl:template name ="DisplayFields">
    <!-- as I don't know what labels to display, just
take the nodename -->
        <xsl:for-each select="*[name()!='invoiceNum'
and name()!='shipToAddress']">
            <xsl:value-of select= "name()"/>
            <xsl:text>: </xsl:text>
            <xsl:value-of select= "."/>
            <br/>
        </xsl:for-each>
    </xsl:template>
```

It’s better to specify what you want to parse:

```
    <xsl:template name ="DisplayFields">
        <xsl:text>sales-date: </xsl:text>
        <xsl:value-of select= "salesDate"/>
        <br/>
        <xsl:text>ship to address: </xsl:text>
        <xsl:value-of select= "shipToAddress"/>
        <br/>
    </xsl:template>
```

Question 41: XSL Mark-up Problem

I have an XML file as shown below:

```
<Paragraph>
  Zamora tells <I>Petroleum Economist</I> that
foreign and private-sector.
</Paragraph>
```

I want to mark it up using the italic tag. With what I have now, I can loop through the Paragraph elements, but I can't get the page to mark up with the <I> element in the right place. This code ignores the "I" tag as it should, but what I am trying to do is mark up the entire paragraph using the child elements as mark up instructions.

```
<xsl:for-each select="Paragraph">
 <xsl:if test="normalize-space(text())">
  <xsl:value-of select="."/><BR/><BR/>
 </xsl:if>
</xsl:for-each>
```

How can I accomplish this?

A: You can try this approach: <xsl:value-of ...> only gives you the value of the node and its children. What you want is to preserve the <I> a tag, which is to insert a node with tag "I" in your result. So you could use <xsl_copy ...> to do that:

```
<?xml version="1.0"?>
<xsl:stylesheet version="1.0"
xmlns:xsl="http://www.w3.org/1999/XSL/Transform">
   <xsl:output method="html" encoding="Windows-1252"
/>
   <xsl:template match="/">
      <html>
         <body>
            <xsl:for-each select="//Paragraph">
               <xsl:apply-templates />
               <BR />
               <BR />
            </xsl:for-each>
         </body>
      </html>
   </xsl:template>
```

```
   <xsl:template match="I">
      <xsl:copy-of select="." />
   </xsl:template>
</xsl:stylesheet>
```

Your final code should look like:

```
<xsl:for-each select="Paragraph">
 <xsl:apply-templates />
 <xsl:if test="normalize-space(text())">
  <xsl:value-of select="."/><BR/><BR/>
 </xsl:if>
</xsl:for-each>

<xsl:template match="I">
  <I><xsl:value-of select="."/></I>
</xsl:template>
```

Question 42: Referring an Outer Element in XSL

My XML looks like this:

```
<root>
  <title>Some title here </title>
    <table>
      .....many table tags here with content....
    </table>

</root>
```

In my XSL, when writing a template for the <table> tag, I need to refer to the <title> tag, and place it inside the <table> tags as follows:

```
<xsl:template match="table">
 <cation><xsl:value-of select="????" />
</caption>
......
</xsl:template>
```

The purpose of this is to make the <caption> tags appear within the <table> tags.
Is it possible to do this? If so, how?

A: For your purpose, you need to use the *parent* axis as show below:

```
<xsl:value-of select=".." />
```

Question 43: Select Node Based on Its Value

If I have the following code:

```
<A>
 <B>first</B>
 <B>second</B> <--want this
 <B>third<B>
</A>
<A>
 <B>fourth</B>
</A>
```

How would I reference the second node based on its 'second' value?

A: You can use the following code:

```
//A/B[text()='second']
```

Question 44: Using XSLT on Multiple XML Files

I have an XSLT file which does some processing on an XML file and it works. However, I need some information out of two XML files at the same time. How do I do this?

A: You can use the xsl:document() function. Here is a link to a basic tutorial:
http://www.w3schools.com/xsl/func_document.asp

Question 45: XSLT Hyperlink

I am trying to render an XML doc to HTML. The XML is like this:

```
<?xml version="1.0"?>
<links>
    <link name="XML Pitstop"
url="http://www.XMLPitstop.com" description="A great
place for XML Demos."/>

</links>
```

I have to display the "name" and "description" attributes as HTML, that works fine using XSLT. But I do not know how to put the URL as a hyperlink on the "name" attribute. How do I do that?

A: You could try:

```
<xsl:element name="A">
<xsl:attribute name="HREF"></xsl:attribute>
</xsl:element>
```

Or you could just write <a href="{URL}">;

Question 46: White Space

I have two projects. One is written in .net (VB.net and ASP.net) the other in VB6 and ASP. Both created an XML document for transformation into HTML. I want to use a non break white space "ie & nbsp" inside the XSL so at the top of my document I have added the following line:

```
<!DOCTYPE xsl:stylesheet <!ENTITY nbsp " ">>
```

This is followed by the rest of my XSL statements:

```
<xsl:stylesheet
xmlns:xsl="http://www.w3.org/1999/XSL/Transform";
version="1.1">

<xsl:output method="xml" indent="yes"/>
.
.
.
etc
```

This all works fine in the .net project. When I do the same in my non .net project xsl file I get this error on the transform statement:

"The stylesheet does not contain a document element. The stylesheet may be empty, or it may not be a well-formed XML document".

Also, when I use an XSL Debugger (a tool you can get from TopXML.com) I get the error message - "The element 'xsl:stylesheet' is used but not declared in the DTD schema". I also get this error when using the stylesheet that works. But when using the transformation, the error messages don't show up. I've done a work around with padding but it still doesn't work. How do I fix this?

A: You don't need to declare it. Just use the built-in entity of & #xa0; (remove space after "&" and before ";" as usual).

Question 47: XML/XSL Generates Bad HTML for Link

In an ASP page, I am using XSL to display links using data from an XML file. It's working fine in IE6 and Netscape 7, but Netscape 6 have a problem because the html that's produced is "not proper" HTML. The problem is that the link does not appear or behave as a link. It's just plain text. Here's the HTML that was produced for a link:

```
<a target="_blank" href="http://www.frallc.com/"
/>Tech-Ops 2004
```

There is no end tag for the <a>, and there's an extra backslash at the end of the beginning <a> tag. Here's the code in my XSL file:

```
<a><xsl:attribute
name="target">_blank</xsl:attribute><xsl:attribute
name="href">http://<xsl:value-of
select="eventurl"/></xsl:attribute></a><xsl:value-of
select="desc"/>
```

And from the XML file:

```
<eventurl>www.frallc.com/</eventurl>
```

I have also tried this in my XSL file:

```
    <xsl:element name="a">
    <xsl:attribute name="href">http://<xsl:value-of
select="eventurl"/></xsl:attribute>
    <xsl:attribute
name="target">_blank</xsl:attribute>
    </xsl:element>
    <xsl:value-of select="desc"/>
```

How do I make this work?

A: You can try this:

```
<a>
<xsl:attribute name="target">_blank</xsl:attribute>
<xsl:attribute name="href">http://<xsl:value-of
select="eventurl"/></xsl:attribute>
```

```
<xsl:value-of select="desc"/>
</a>
```

Note: line breaks are added for clarity only.

http://www.mcgonagall-online.org.uk
http://www.napitalia.org.uk
http://www.leicesteryha.org.uk

Question 48: XSL for XML Database

I have the following simple XML database:

```
<?xml version="1.0"?>
<?xml-stylesheet href = "sample.xsl" type =
"text/xsl"?>
<!DOCTYPE Quiz SYSTEM "sample.dtd">

<Quiz Status="NewVersion">
   <QuestionsAnswers QuestionNumber="1"

        Question="1

        Answer1 ="correct"
        Answer2 ="correct"
        Answer3 ="correct"
        Answer4 ="correct"
 />

</Quiz>
```

The following DTD describes the Database:

```
<?xml version="1.0"?>
<!ELEMENT Quiz (QuestionsAnswers*)>
  <!ATTLIST Quiz
    Status (NewVersion | UpdatedVersion |
CourtesyCopy) #REQUIRED>
  <!ELEMENT QuestionsAnswers EMPTY>
  <!ATTLIST QuestionAnswers
     QuestionNumber CDATA #REQUIRED
     Question CDATA #REQUIRED
     Answer1 CDATA #REQUIRED
     Answer2 CDATA #REQUIRED
     Answer3 CDATA #REQUIRED
```

```
    Answer4 CDATA #REQUIRED
    >
```

I am trying to create an XSL style sheet that will display the question and then underneath this the four answers each with a corresponding radio button. All I have is the following:

```
<?xml version = "1.0"?>
<xsl:stylesheet xmlns:xsl =
"http://www.w3c.org/1999/XSL/Transform"; version =
"1.0">
<xsl:output method = "html"/>

<xsl:template match = "Quiz">

<body bgcolor = "#FFDDFF">
<p><xsl:apply-templates/></p>
</body>
</xsl:template>
</xsl:stylesheet>
```

I really would appreciate any help because my XSL skills are basic.

A: I think your XML is a little but rusty and not thoroughly expressed. You've left yourself no way to iterate through your attributes in a meaningful way without examining the name of each attribute, which just makes it all harder. You've included data in the attribute names themselves. That is bad form practice. Something like the one below will be better:

```
<?xml version="1.0"?>
<quiz status="New Version">
  <item number="1">
    <question>When did Columbus discover America?
      <answer choice="A">1492</answer>
      <answer choice="B">Columbus didn't discover
America, Indians did.</answer>
      <answer choice="C">Columbus was a putz: he
thought he was in India.</answer>
      <answer choice="D">Columbus didn't discover
America, native Americans did.</answer>
    </question>
  </item>
</quiz>
```

Now, you can use an XSL template to select the answer nodes and output whatever you want. If you put more thought into the XML (i.e., structuring the data) and how you're going to use it, the XSL will be less of a problem.

Question 49: Using XML+XSLT+CSS

I have an XML file that references an XSLT style sheet which turns the results into a sorted table. This part works fine. I would like to further tweak the results by adding a reference to a CSS file so the sorted table results could be in a different font, color, etc. IE 6.1 gives me errors when I try to put <link> or <style> elements right into the XSL.

Where do I put the link to the CSS file? I have tried just about everything I can think of, and none of it works.

A: You can try this in XSLT:

```
<html>
<head>
<link .... />
</head>
```

Question 50: When Using a Test With an 'or'

This is the code I have:

```
<xsl:choose>
    <xsl:when test="//document/menu/@selectopt =
'Modify'">
```

I want this to work if the //document/menu/@selectopt = 'Modify' OR //document/menu/@selectopt = 'Delete'.

How can I do this?

A: I think this is what you want:

```
<xsl:choose>

   <xsl:when test="//document/menu/@selectopt =
'Modify'">
      Code in here
   </xsl:when>

   <xsl:when test="//document/menu/@selectopt =
'Delete'>
      Code in here
   </xsl:when>

   <xsl:otherwise>
      Code in here
   </xsl:otherwise>

</xsl:choose>
```

Actually, it is possible to use "or" within an if or when statement in XSL such as :

```
<xsl:when test="($variable= 1) Or ($variable=2)">

</xsl:when>
```

Question 51: XSLT Output – Well-Formed HTML

I am performing XSLT transformations on templates that are built using well-formed HTML, i.e., all tags are closed like this: <br/>.

The transformation works fine, but the HTML output generated seems to have removed the closing tags from my <br/> nodes (making them <br>), and now the output is not well-formed. This means I cannot add the resulting HTML data to a further XML message without having to use a routine to run through adding all of the closing tags back in again.

Am I missing something?

A: If you want to generate HTML that is also XML, then you have to generate XHTML. If this is the case, make sure the method attribute for the <xsl:output> is "xml", and have the appropriate document type. For example, your style sheet could begin like this:

```
<?xml version="1.0" encoding="UTF-8"?>
<xsl:stylesheet version="1.0"
xmlns:xsl="http://www.w3.org/1999/XSL/Transform">
    <xsl:output method="xml" indent="yes" cdata-
section-elements="script style" doctype-public="-
//W3C//DTD XHTML 1.0 Strict//EN"/>
```

For more info on XHTML, see: http://www.w3.org/MarkUp/#xhtml1.

Question 52: XSL: Testing for Existence

How do I go about testing for the existence of a value in my XML? For example:

```
<person>
<name value="Peter">
<address>75 Hunts Street</address>
</name>
<name value="Andrew">
<address></address>
</name>
<name>
<address>45 Main</address>
</name>
</person>
```

In the above, how could I go about using the "for-each" to only display on values but not empties?

A: If the values were empty, nothing would be displayed. The way you can test if something exists would be something like this:

```
<xsl:if test="Address!=''">
  <xsl:value-of select="Address"/>
</xsl:if>
```

This would only display the value if it existed. Another way to check would be to use content-length codes. For example:

```
<xsl:if test="content-length(Address)>0">
```

This code checks if the length of the content is greater than 0.

Question 53: Pass Value and ID into ASP Script

This is the XSL I have. What I need to do is pass the ID as well as the value back to my ASP script. At the moment it passes the value only. I'm trying to extend someone's code. This someone has left the company. The template is of the form ID Value where “only Value” is displayed in the select drop down List.

```
<xsl:template name="position">
    <select class="sys_text" name="position">
      <option value="none">(select)</option>
      <xsl:for-each select="root/position/item">
        <option>
          <xsl:attribute name="value"><xsl:value-of
select="@value"/></xsl:attribute>
          <xsl:value-of select="@value"/>
        </option>
      </xsl:for-each>
    </select>
</xsl:template>
```

A: The simplest way to do this is to pass them both in the value and split them on the ASP page. They will be in the format ID,Value in the Request.Form on the next page.

XSL:

```
<xsl:template name="position">
    <select class="sys_text" name="position">
      <option value="none">(select)</option>
      <xsl:for-each select="root/position/item">
        <option>
          <xsl:attribute name="value"><xsl:value-of
select="@id"/>,<xsl:value-of
select="@value"/></xsl:attribute>
          <xsl:value-of select="@value"/>
        </option>
      </xsl:for-each>
    </select>
    </xsl:template>
```

ASP:

```
Dim varId, varValue, both
'split the comma delimited  contents into 2 element
array
both = split(Request.Form("position"),",")

'put the contents in the correct variables
varId = both(0)
varValue = both(1)
```

That is one way to ID, probably the easiest as it requires no client scripting but keeps the ID and value pair together. The XSL is assuming that the ID is an attribute just like the value.

Question 54: Display Document on Client Side

I have a few XML/XSL related questions. I have an ASP application which calls a dll created in VB. I created an XML Document using the DOM in the VB6 dll and return this XML document back to the calling function in ASP. I want to display this document on the client side. There is a saved XSL sheet which deals with the formatting in the same folder.

I have the following questions:

1. Can I display this XML document without having to save it first?
2. How can I display it using the XSL style sheet?
3. Can I use the Document.write xmlDoc method to display the data from inside my VBscript Sub?

I don't want to save this XML document at this point. I would like to do it later when I need to save it as a PDF file. Are there available sample codes I could look at to see how this is done?

A: To answer to your questions in the same order:

1. Yes. Use the following:

```
response.write mydocument.xml;
```

2. To transform the document, use another IXMLDOmDocument to load the XSLT and create an XSLProcessor to transform:

```
    ... original document creation code...
    myXSLDocument =
Server.CreateObject("Msxml2.FreeThreadedDOMDocument40
")
    myXSLDocument.load("myxsl.xsl");
    myXSLT =
Server.CreateObject("Msxml2.XSLTemplate40")
    myXSLT.stylesheet = myXSLDocument
    xslProc = myXSLT.createProcessor()

    xslProc.input = myXMLDocument ' your document you
create b4!!

    xslProc.transform

    response.write xslProc.output
```

3. On erm. No, you can't use it to display data. Use response.write from ASP instead.

If you are a beginner, the MSXML documentation could help you a lot. Go to: http://msdn.microsoft.com/downloads/sample.asp?url=/msdn-files/027/001/766/msdncompositedoc.xml for the download or use MSDN on Microsoft's site to look up functionality.

Question 55: Dynamic XSL

Is there any way to send variables to an XSL file, so I can pull out records based on some ID? Usually I just use the DOM method for this, but I am just wondering if there is any other way?

A: This is what you are looking for:

```
Dim xslt As New Msxml2.XSLTemplate
Dim xslDoc As New Msxml2.FreeThreadedDOMDocument
Dim xmlDoc As New Msxml2.DOMDocument
Dim xslProc As IXSLProcessor
xslDoc.async = False
xslDoc.Load "sample.xsl"
Set xslt.stylesheet = xslDoc
xmlDoc.async = False
xmlDoc.Load "books.xml"
Set xslProc = xslt.createProcessor()
xslProc.input = xmlDoc
xslProc.addParameter "param1", "Hello"
xslProc.Transform
MsgBox xslProc.output
Sample.xsl

<xsl:stylesheet
xmlns:xsl="http://www.w3.org/1999/XSL/Transform";
version="1.0">
   <xsl:output method="html"/>
   <xsl:param name="param1"/>
  <xsl:template match="/">
      The parameter value was: <xsl:value-of
select="$param1"/>
  </xsl:template>
</xsl:stylesheet>
```

Question 56: XSL Loop

I'm using XSL to dynamically populate a drop down list. The XML is basically a list of names with an ID number. I can populate the list properly if I know how many entries are in the XML document. I also need to use a loop so it stops making the drop down list when the id = "x" marks the end of the file.

Here is my code so far:

```
 <xsl:element name="Select">
                       <xsl:attribute
name="NAME">status</xsl:attribute>
                       <xsl:attribute
name="size">1</xsl:attribute>

                                   <xsl:element
name="option">
                                       <xsl:attribute
name="value"><xsl:value-of
select="ID"/></xsl:attribute>
                                       <xsl:attribute
name="selected"/>
                                       <xsl:for-each
select="details/person[id= 1]">
                                       <xsl:value-of
select="FirstName"/> <xsl:value-of
select="LastName"/>
                                       </xsl:for-each>
                                   </xsl:element>
                                   <xsl:element
name="option">
                                       <xsl:attribute
name="value"><xsl:value-of
select="ID"/></xsl:attribute>
                                       <xsl:attribute
name="selected"/>
                                   <xsl:for-each
select="details/person[id= 2]">
                                       <xsl:value-of
select="FirstName"/> <xsl:value-of
select="LastName"/>
                                   </xsl:for-each>
                                   </xsl:element>
                                   <xsl:element
name="option">
                                       <xsl:attribute
```

```
name="value"><xsl:value-of
select="ID"/></xsl:attribute>
                                    <xsl:for-each
select="details/person[id= 3]">
                                    <xsl:value-of
select="FirstName"/> <xsl:value-of
select="LastName"/>
                                    </xsl:for-each>
                                </xsl:element>
                </xsl:element>
```

A: It should be possible with <xsl:for-each>.

```
<xsl:for-each select="details/person">
  <xsl:element name="option">
    <xsl:attribute name="value" select="ID"/>
    <xsl:attribute name="selected"/>
    <xsl:value-of select="concat(FirstName, ' ',
LastName)"/>
  </xsl:element>
</xsl:for-each>
```

If the attribute for "selected" is not always there, then you could add an <xsl:if>.

Question 57: XSL: Change Element Value into Attribute Value

I have something like this:

```
<name>
  <first>Joe</first>
  <last>Soap</last>
</name>
I want to convert this to:
<name first="Joe" last="Soap"/>
```

I've tried:

```
<xsl:text><name first="</xsl:text>
<xsl:value-of select="first"/>
<xsl:text>" last="</xsl:text>
<xsl:value-of select="last"/>
<xsl:text>"/></xsl:text>
```

However, this is treated as element content as opposed to an Element. How do I change element value into an attribute value?

A: You can use this:

```
<name first="{first}" last="{last}"/>
```

the bit inside the "{}" is an XPath statement.

Question 58: To Get the id="C" or id="E"

I have the following XML code:

```
<?xml version="1.0"?>
<Report>
    <Settings width="100%"></Settings>
    <Heading>
        <Title>My Report Title</Title>
        <Columns>
            <Column id="A" width="11%" align="right"
title="Column-A"/>
            <Column id="B" title="Column-B"/>
            <Column id="C" title="Column-C"/>
            <Column id="D" title="Column-D"/>
            <Column id="E" title="Column-E"/>
        </Columns>
    </Heading>
    <Data>
        <Row> /Report/Heading/Columns/Column(ID)
            <Cell column="A"
href="http://mylink";>MyCellData-A</Cell>
            <Cell column="B"
href="http://mylink";>MyCellData-B</Cell>
            <Cell column="C"
href="http://mylink";>MyCellData-C</Cell>
            <Cell column="D"
href="http://mylink";>MyCellData-D</Cell>
            <Cell column="E"
href="http://mylink";>MyCellData-E</Cell>
        </Row>
    </Data>
    <Footer>
        <FooterComment>This report is not designed to
be printed</FooterComment>
    </Footer>
</Report>
```

I would like to do the following:

```
<xsl:value-of
     select="/Report/Headings/Columns/Column/@id"/>
```

The problem is that this will only get the first instance of the @id property. What happens if I want to get the id="C" or id="E"? Is there a way of matching specific values of the id property? I want to be able to read the width property of a specific instance of /Report/Heading/Column/Columns, based on the value of id.

A: In this situation you need to use "[]" to get the result you want. So the direct answer to your question is:

```
/Report/Headings/Columns/Column[@id='A']/@id
```

I think of the "[]" to mean "where". You can have more complex XPath with more than one pair of "[]". The other main thing to know is that to get say the third element you do something like /some/path/to/list/element[3]. Or you can do something like this:

```
<xsl:stylesheet version="1.0"
xmlns:xsl="http://www.w3.org/1999/XSL/Transform">
<xsl:template match="/">
testing
<xsl:for-each
select="Report/Heading/Columns/Column[@id = 'A']">
<xsl:value-of select="@width"/> <!--this will output
the value of the with attribute-->
</xsl:for-each>
</xsl:template>
</xsl:stylesheet>
```

Question 59: Variables in XSL

Can you use variables in XSL? I want to loop through a list of objects, and give each object a unique numeric value for use in HTML. I wanted to do this through variables. Is there another way?

A: Use position().

```
<xsl:for-each select="object">
<xsl:value-of select="position()"/><br/>
</xsl:value-of>
```

Position() will return where you are in your list of nodes.

Question 60: Putting XSL: Value -of in Text Box

I'm trying to use XSL to take a value from an XML document and place it into an HTML text box; however, I can't get it in the text box. For example:

```
<input type="text" name="textfield6">
<xsl:value-of select="/details/address"/>

        </input>
```

How can I do it correctly?

A: Use the attribute function.

```
<input name="whatever"><xsl:attribute
name="value"><xsl:value-of
select="whatever"/></xsl:attribute></input>
```

This will send output in the HTML:

```
<input name="whatever" value="whatever the value was
in the xsl-value of">;
```

Question 61: Passing Parameters to XSL Doc

Is it possible to pass name value pairs to an XSL doc, and then access these values using <xsl:param>? I have the code set up to do the transform server side or client side as I've been testing both methods. How can I do this?

A: It seems that for the client side, processing passing parameters is not possible or obvious; most codes are on the server side.

On the server side, the way to pass parameters to the style sheet depends very much on what is controlling the XSL, e.g., Java, Perl, ASP. Usually the function to call the style sheet will allow you to pass the parameters to it. The XSL code I have posted in the part is what picks up these parameters.

At the top of the XSL you declare the parameters. This needs to be done as a top level element, i.e., right after the opening <xsl:stylesheet> or <xsl:transform> tag.

```
<xsl:param name="color"/>
```

So if you passed a parameter named color from your script it would pick this up and store it in $color. Think of it as a global variable. Then if you wanted to print this value later you reference it like this:

```
<xsl:value-of select="$color"/>
```

To finish off with, if you wanted a default value for the parameter, when a value isn't given you could do something like:

```
<xsl:param name="color">red</xsl:param>
```

So, if you passed color as being blue, this would override the value of red.

Question 62: XSL or DTD

I just started trying to learn XML. I understand about the syntax of tags, etc., but I was wondering if you're using an XSLT file to transform your XML, do you need a DTD? If so, why is this?

A: The XSL style sheet doesn't always need the XML file to come with a DTD. In fact, as you can imagine, it slows things down quite a bit. Without it you can't really trust the XML. So if your XSL file assumes that there is an element <title> in every <book> it won't be able to throw an error if it's not there. But if you had a DTD with the XML it would make sure that every <book> did have a <title> before the XSL started to do anything.

Always set the rule in using a server to process XML. Don't include the DTD because you can trust your own code. In writing XSL for client side processing always give the DTD to the user, because they might not trust your xml and they probably won't notice the extra CPU time taken by checking the xml.

Question 63: Variable Scope Help Needed in XSLT

How would I create a variable in an XSLT stylesheet, that would be visible globally, but also able to be set to different values several times? For example:

```
<xsl:choose>
<xsl:when test="'1'">
<xsl:variable name="var" select="'1'"/>
</xsl:when>
<xsl:otherwise>
<xsl:variable name="var" select="'2'"/>
</xsl:otherwise>
</xsl:choose>
```

I want to be able to access "var" outside of the choose block, but apparently, it is only visible inside the chosen block. Is there a way I can do this?

A: Put the "choose block" inside a function.

```
<xsl:template name="myFunc">
  <xsl:choose>
    <xsl:when test="'1'">
      <xsl:value-of select="'1'"
    </xsl:when
    ...
    ...
  </xsl:choose>
</xsl:template>
```

and then in the rest of the code.

```
<xsl:variable name="test">
<xsl:call-template name="muFunc"/>
</xsl:variable>
```

Then you can use $test.

Question 64: Finding an Element

I am trying to convert some XML to HTML using XSL. One thing I want to check is to see if an element exists, and if so display its value, and if it does not exist, to display something like a dash (-). I know how to check if the element is empty but not if it exists within the document or not. Is this possible? How is it done?

A: The count() function should do it. For example:

```
<?xml version="1.0" encoding="UTF-8"?>
<?xml-stylesheet type="text/xsl"
href="./missingtag.xsl" ?>
<books>
    <book>
        <title>book1</title>
        <author>manx</author>
    </book>
    <book>
        <title>book2</title>
    </book>
</books>
```

It could be transformed with this:

```
<?xml version="1.0" encoding="UTF-8"?>
<xsl:stylesheet version="1.0"
xmlns:xsl="http://www.w3.org/1999/XSL/Transform";
xmlns:fo="http://www.w3.org/1999/XSL/Format";>
    <xsl:template match="/">
        <HTML>
            <table>
                <xsl:apply-templates select="books"/>
            </table>
        </HTML>
    </xsl:template>

    <xsl:template match="books">
            <xsl:apply-templates select="book"/>
    </xsl:template>

    <xsl:template match="book">
        <tr>
        <td><xsl:value-of select="title"/></td>
        <xsl:choose>
            <xsl:when test="count(author)=0">
                <td>-</td>
            </xsl:when>
            <xsl:otherwise>
                <td><xsl:value-of
select="author"/></td>
            </xsl:otherwise>
        </xsl:choose>
        </tr>
    </xsl:template>

</xsl:stylesheet>
```

Question 65: XSL Count

I would like to know how to count the number of nodes in an XML file, and return the value to an ASP file?

A: Let say we have the following catalog.xml file:

```
<catalog>
  <book id="bk101">
    <author>Who, Mat</author>
    <title>XML Developer's Guide</title>
    <genre>Computer</genre>
    <price>44.95</price>
    <publish_date>2000-10-01</publish_date>
    <description>An in-depth look at creating
applications with XML.</description>
   </book>
   <book id="bk102">
     <author>Rall, Kim</author>
     <title>Midnight Rain</title>
     <genre>Fantasy</genre>
     <price>5.95</price>
     <publish_date>2000-12-16</publish_date>
     <description> ... become queen of the
world.</description>
   </book>
</catalog>
```

There are two possible answers to your question.

1. Using catalog.xsl file and catalog.asp file to transform the XML file to what you need. There is a function count() in XSLT which will do the task for counting how many books we have.

catalog.xsl:

```
<xsl:stylesheet version="1.0"
xmlns:xsl="http://www.w3.org/1999/XSL/Transform";>
<xsl:output method="html"/>
   <xsl:template match="/">
     <html>
    <body>
        Book counted: <xsl:value-of
select="count(//book)"/>
    </body>
      </html>
```

```
   </xsl:template>
</xsl:stylesheet>
```

```
catalog1.asp:

<%
'Load the XML
set oXmlDoc =
Server.CreateObject("MSXML2.DOMdocument")
oXmlDoc.async = false
oXmLDoc.load(Server.MapPath("catalog.xml"))

'Load the XSL
set oXslDoc =
Server.CreateObject("MSXML2.DOMdocument")
oXslDoc.async = false
oXslDoc.load(Server.MapPath("catalog.xsl"))

'Transform the file
Response.Write(oXmlDoc.transformNode(oXslDoc))
%>
```

This transformation will display the following:

```
"Books counted: 2"
```

2. Using ASP with XML DOM specification, there are some things to know:

* getElementsByTagName - returns a collection of elements that have the specified name (e.g., "book", "author", etc.)
* <name_of_collection>.length - indicates the number of items in the collection // that is in your case count number of the nodes
* <name_of_collection>.item(i) - i-th element of the collection, index start from 0
* <XML_DOM_Node>.text - string; contains the text content of the node or the concatenated text representing this node and its descendants:

```
catalog2.asp
<%
Dim objXmlDoc
Dim objNodeList
Set objXmlDoc = CreateObject("Msxml2.DOMDocument")
objXmlDoc.async = False
objXmlDoc.load(Server.MapPath("catalog.xml"))
```

```
Set objNodeList =
objXmlDoc.getElementsByTagName("book")
For i=0 To (objNodeList.length -1)
  Response.write (objNodeList.item(i).text)
  Response.write "<br>"
Next

%>
```

Question 66: Transfer XML into XSLT

I have an input XML with different tags. I would like to select the tag I wanted and parse to the text output file. Here is the input XML files:

```
<FIXML xmlns="http://www.fixprotocol.org/FIXML-4-4"
r="20030618" s="20040109" v="4.4" xr="FIA" xv="1">
<Batch>
<SecListUpd BizDt="2006-04-24" RptID="8705349"
UpdActn="M">
<Pty ID="XASE" R="22">
<Sub ID="2001-06-20" Typ="27"></Sub>
</Pty>
</SecListUpd>

<SecDefUpd BizDt="2006-04-24" Ccy="USD"
RptID="8026163" UpdActn="M">
<Pty ID="XASE" R="22">
<Sub ID="2001-06-20" Typ="27"></Sub>
</Pty>
</SecDefUpd>

<SecDef BizDt="2006-04-24" Ccy="USD" RptID="23743">
<Pty ID="XASE" R="22">
<Sub ID="2001-06-20" Typ="27"></Sub>
</Pty>
</SecDef>

<SecList BizDt="2006-04-24" RptID="8469055">
<Instrmt CFI="OCECPN" ID="EQ" MMY="200605"
MatDt="2006-05-12" Src="J" StrkPx="1480"
StrkQt="1480.00" Sym="CBP">
<Evnt Dt="2006-02-11" EventTyp="5"></Evnt>
</Instrmt>
</SecList>
```

```
</Batch>
</FIXML>
```

If I only want to parse the tag = SecDefUpd or SecDef, what do I need to change with my XSLT? The following is my XSLT:

```
<?xml version="1.0"?>
<xsl:stylesheet version="1.0"
xmlns:xsl="http://www.w3.org/1999/XSL/Transform"
xmlns:a="http://www.fixprotocol.org/FIXML-4-4">

<xsl:template match="/">
<xsl:apply-templates
select="a:FIXML/a:Batch/child::*"/>
</xsl:template>

<xsl:template match="*">
<xsl:for-each select="descendant-or-self::*">
<xsl:for-each select="attribute::*">
<xsl:value-of select="."/>
<xsl:text>|</xsl:text>
</xsl:for-each>
</xsl:for-each><xsl:text>
</xsl:text> </xsl:template>
</xsl:stylesheet>
```

A: You can change it as follows:

```
<xsl:apply-templates
select="a:FIXML/a:Batch/child::*"/>
```

into:

```
<xsl:apply-templates select="a:FIXML/a:Batch/*[local-
name()='SecDefUpd' or local-name()='SecDef']"/>
```

Question 67: A Special Sum Question

How do you handle a special sum question or query and translate it into an XML/XSLT function?

A: You can start by trying this:

```
<xsl:key name="EDI" match="Detail"
use="concat(Entity, ':', Quantity/HourlyBeginTime,
Quantity/HourlyEndTime)"/>

<xsl:template match="/EDI/Detail">

<xsl:apply-templates select="key('EDI',
concat(Entity,':',Quantity/HourlyBeginTime,
Quantity/HourlyEndTime))" mode="Sum"/>
</xsl:template>

<xsl:template match="Detail" mode="Sum">
<xsl:variable name="thekey" select="concat(Entity,
':', Quantity/HourlyBeginTime,
Quantity/HourlyEndTime)"/>
<xsl:value-of
select="sum(/EDI/Detail/Quantity/HourlyQuantity[conca
t(../../Entity, ':',../HourlyBeginTime,
../HourlyEndTime) = $thekey])"/>
<xsl:text>
</xsl:text>
</xsl:template>
```

And if you got a chance to transform the attached XML:

```
<EDI>
- <Detail>
<UnitOfMeasure>KW1</UnitOfMeasure>
<DirectionOfFlow>U</DirectionOfFlow>
<Entity>Cargill</Entity>
<EntityQualifier>ZEW</EntityQualifier>
<QuantityQualifier>Z05</QuantityQualifier>
- <Quantity>
<HourlyBeginTime>2006-07-
01T04:00:00</HourlyBeginTime>
<HourlyEndTime>2006-07-01T22:00:00</HourlyEndTime>
<HourlyQuantity>-19000000</HourlyQuantity>
</Quantity>
```

```
- <Quantity>
<HourlyBeginTime>2006-07-
01T22:00:00</HourlyBeginTime>
<HourlyEndTime>2006-07-02T00:00:00</HourlyEndTime>
<HourlyQuantity>-1000000</HourlyQuantity>
</Quantity>
- <Quantity>
<HourlyBeginTime>2007-07-
01T04:00:00</HourlyBeginTime>
<HourlyEndTime>2007-07-01T22:00:00</HourlyEndTime>
<HourlyQuantity>15000000</HourlyQuantity>
</Quantity>
</Detail>
- <Detail>
<UnitOfMeasure>KW1</UnitOfMeasure>
<DirectionOfFlow>D</DirectionOfFlow>
<Entity>Cargill</Entity>
<EntityQualifier>ZEW</EntityQualifier>
<QuantityQualifier>Z05</QuantityQualifier>
- <Quantity>
<HourlyBeginTime>2006-07-
01T22:00:00</HourlyBeginTime>
<HourlyEndTime>2006-07-02T00:00:00</HourlyEndTime>
<HourlyQuantity>5990000</HourlyQuantity>
</Quantity>
- <Quantity>
<HourlyBeginTime>2006-07-
02T00:00:00</HourlyBeginTime>
<HourlyEndTime>2006-07-02T04:00:00</HourlyEndTime>
<HourlyQuantity>0</HourlyQuantity>
</Quantity>
</Detail>
- <Detail>
<UnitOfMeasure>KW1</UnitOfMeasure>
<DirectionOfFlow>D</DirectionOfFlow>
<Entity>Accord</Entity>
<EntityQualifier>ZEW</EntityQualifier>
<QuantityQualifier>Z05</QuantityQualifier>
- <Quantity>
<HourlyBeginTime>2006-07-
01T04:00:00</HourlyBeginTime>
<HourlyEndTime>2006-07-02T04:00:00</HourlyEndTime>
<HourlyQuantity>84000000</HourlyQuantity>
</Quantity>
</Detail>
</EDI>
```

I am using the XSLT:

```
<?xml version="1.0" encoding="UTF-8"?>
<?xml-stylesheet type="text/xsl" href=".xslt"?>
<xsl:stylesheet version="1.0"
xmlns:xsl="http://www.w3.org/1999/XSL/Transform"
xmlns:msxsl="urn:schemas-microsoft-com:xslt"
xmlns:vbs="urn:schemas-sqlxml-org:vbs">

<xsl:key name="EDI" match="Detail"
use="concat(Entity, ':', Quantity/HourlyBeginTime,
Quantity/HourlyEndTime)"/>

<xsl:template match="/EDI">
<xsl:apply-templates select="Detail[count(.|
key('EDI',concat(Entity,':',Quantity/HourlyBeginTime,
Quantity/HourlyEndTime))[1])=1]" />
</xsl:template>

<xsl:template match="Detail">
<xsl:variable name="thekey" select="concat(Entity,
':', Quantity/HourlyBeginTime,
Quantity/HourlyEndTime)"/>
<xsl:value-of
select="sum(/EDI/Detail/Quantity/HourlyQuantity[conca
t(../../Entity, ':', ../HourlyBeginTime,
../HourlyEndTime) = $thekey])"/>
</xsl:template>
</xsl:stylesheet>
```

You'll have the grouped result by "Entity"," HourlyBeginTime", and "HourlyEndTime":

```
QTY+:Test -19000000
QTY+:Test 4990000
QTY+:Test 84000000
```

If the result is missing QTY: 15000000 that is a Muenchian Method group, see the attached version. It is in a more verbose form to better demonstrate how grouping works.

```
<?xml version="1.0" encoding="UTF-8"?>
<xsl:stylesheet version="1.0"
xmlns:xsl="http://www.w3.org/1999/XSL/Transform">
<xsl:key name="EDI" match="Detail/Quantity"
use="concat(../Entity, ':', HourlyBeginTime,
HourlyEndTime)"/>

<xsl:template match="/EDI">
<xsl:for-each select="Detail/Quantity">
```

```
<xsl:variable name="key"
select="concat(../Entity,':',HourlyBeginTime,HourlyEn
dTime)"/>

<xsl:variable name="group" select="key('EDI',
$key)"/>

<xsl:if test="generate-id(.) = generate-id( $group[1]
) ">

<xsl:variable name="quantity"
select="sum($group/HourlyQuantity)"/>
<xsl:value-of select="concat(../Entity, ':',
string($quantity), '&#10;')"/>

</xsl:if>

</xsl:for-each>
</xsl:template>
</xsl:stylesheet>
```

And if you are interested in two level grouping, of which the first group by Entity and the other Group by Entity + HourlyBeginTime + HourlyEndTime such as:

```
Output:
Cargill:
QTY+: -19000000
QTY+: 4990000
QTY: 15000000
Accord:
QTY+: 84000000
```

You can easily do 2 level grouping using two keys and two nested loop. Here is a solution in XSLT 2.0 that takes advantage of for-each-group. But you can't use stylesheet version="2.0" so xslt can not contain xsl:for-each-group. Trying to do it with version 1.0:

```
<xml version="1.0" encoding="UTF-8">
<?xml-stylesheet type="text/xsl" ><xsl:stylesheet
version="1.0"
xmlns:xsl="http://www.w3.org/1999/XSL/Transform" >

<xsl:key name="EDI" match="Detail"
use="concat(Entity, ':', Quantity/HourlyBeginTime,
```

```
Quantity/HourlyEndTime)"/>
<xsl:key name="Group-Entity" match="Detail"
use="Entity"/>
<xsl:template match="/EDI">
<xsl:for-each select="Detail">
<xsl:variable name="key2" select="Entity"/>
<xsl:variable name="group2" select="key('Group-
Entity', $key2)"/>
<xsl:if test="generate-id(.) = generate-id(
$group2[1] ) ">
<xsl:variable name="groupedEntity" select="Entity" />
<xsl:for-each select="../Detail">
<xsl:variable name="key"
select="concat($groupedEntity,':',Quantity/HourlyBegi
nTime,Quantity/HourlyEndTime)"/>
<xsl:variable name="group" select="key('EDI',
$key)"/>
<xsl:if test="generate-id(.) = generate-id( $group[1]
) ">
<xsl:variable name="quantity"
select="sum($group/HourlyQuantity)"/>
</xsl:if>
</xsl:for-each>
</xsl:if>
</xsl:for-each>
```

And if the sum is zero, try doing this:

```
<?xml version="1.0" encoding="UTF-8"?>
<xsl:stylesheet version="1.0"
xmlns:xsl="http://www.w3.org/1999/XSL/Transform">
<xsl:key name="EDI" match="Detail/Quantity"
use="concat(../Entity, ':', HourlyBeginTime,
HourlyEndTime)"/>
<xsl:key name="Group-Entity" match="Detail"
use="Entity"/>
<xsl:template match="/EDI">
<xsl:for-each select="Detail">
<xsl:variable name="key2" select="Entity"/>
<xsl:variable name="group2" select="key('Group-
Entity', $key2)"/>
<xsl:if test="generate-id(.) = generate-id(
$group2[1] ) ">
<xsl:value-of select="concat(Entity, ':&#10;')"/>
<xsl:variable name="groupedEntity" select="Entity"/>
<xsl:for-each select="$group2/Quantity">
<xsl:variable name="key"
select="concat($groupedEntity,':',HourlyBeginTime,Hou
```

```
rlyEndTime)"/>
<xsl:variable name="group" select="key('EDI',
$key)"/>
<xsl:if test="generate-id(.) = generate-id( $group[1]
) ">
<xsl:variable name="quantity"
select="sum($group/HourlyQuantity)"/>
<xsl:value-of select="concat(' ', $quantity,
'&#10;')"/>
</xsl:if>
</xsl:for-each>
</xsl:if>
</xsl:for-each>
</xsl:template>
</xsl:stylesheet>
```

Question 68: Keeping Track of Data

I am using XSLT to format an XML file called orders.xml. I need to collect the 'invoices_rec' elements for each customer with the same invoiceNum. I am using a loop but I need to find a way to save the last invoice number in order to see if it has changed, so that I can compare it with the new invoiceNum.

I am using this variable:

```
<xsl:variable name="last_invoice_number"
select="invoices/invoices_rec/invoiceNum"/>
```

I am using this test, but it does not work:

```
<!-- Check that invoiceNum has changed -->
<xsl:if test="invoiceNum != $last_invoice_number">
code here
</xsl:if>
```

Here is another version:

```
<?xml version="1.0" encoding="ISO-8859-1"?>
<xsl:stylesheet version="1.0"
xmlns:xsl="http://www.w3.org/1999/XSL/Transform">
<xsl:template match="/database">
```

```
<html>
<body>
<h2>All Customer Invoices</h2>
<title>All Customer Invoices</title>

<!-- display FIRST customer details -->
<p />Ship to:<br/><br/>
<p /><xsl:value-of
select="invoices/invoices_rec/contactName"/><br />
<xsl:value-of
select="invoices/invoices_rec/shipToAddress"/><br />
<xsl:value-of
select="invoices/invoices_rec/shipToCity"/><br />
<xsl:value-of
select="invoices/invoices_rec/shipToState"/><br />
<xsl:value-of
select="invoices/invoices_rec/shipToZip"/><br />

<!-- display FIRST customer invoice details -->
<br/><p />INVOICE NUMBER: <xsl:value-of
select="invoices/invoices_rec/invoiceNum"/>
<p />SALES DATE: <xsl:value-of
select="invoices/invoices_rec/salesDate"/><br/><br/>

<!-- Capture and store FIRST invoiceNum -->
<xsl:variable name="last_invoice_number"
select="invoices/invoices_rec/invoiceNum"/>

<!-- display table headers -->
<table border="1">
<tr bgcolor="#9acd32">
<th>Product ID</th>
<th>Product Name</th>
<th>Product Description</th>
<th>Quantity</th>
<th>Unit Price</th>
<th>Extended Price</th>
</tr>

<!-- Start main loop here -->
<xsl:for-each select="invoices/invoices_rec">

<!-- Check that customer has changed -->
<xsl:if test="invoiceNum != $last_invoice_number">

<!-- display NEW customer details, since new customer
-->
<p />Ship to:<br/><br/>
```

```
<p /><xsl:value-of select="contactName"/><br />
<xsl:value-of select="shipToAddress"/><br />
<xsl:value-of select="shipToCity"/><br />
<xsl:value-of select="shipToState"/><br />
<xsl:value-of select="shipToZip"/><br />

<!-- display NEW customer invoice details -->
<br/><p />INVOICE NUMBER: <xsl:value-of
select="invoiceNum"/>
<p />SALES DATE: <xsl:value-of
select="salesDate"/><br/><br/>

<!-- display new table headers -->
<table border="1">
<tr bgcolor="#9acd32">
<th>Product ID</th>
<th>Product Name</th>
<th>Product Description</th>
<th>Quantity</th>
<th>Unit Price</th>
<th>Extended Price</th>
</tr>
</table>

<!-- Store last invoiceNum -->
<xsl:for-each select="invoiceNum">
<xsl:variable name="last_invoice_number" select="."/>

</xsl:for-each>

</xsl:if>

<!-- display PRODUCT details in a table -->
<tr>
<td><xsl:value-of select="ProductID"/></td>
<td><xsl:value-of select="ProductName"/></td>
<td><xsl:value-of select="ProductDescription"/></td>
<td><xsl:value-of select="Quantity"/></td>
<td><xsl:value-of select="UnitPrice"/></td>
<td><xsl:value-of select="ExtendedPrice"/></td>
</tr>

</xsl:for-each>

<!-- Close last table -->
</table><br/><br/>

</body>
```

```
</html>

</xsl:template>
</xsl:stylesheet>
```

A: This is a basic grouping problem. Please use the attached solution to guide you in the right direction. And if you encounter this condition:

```
<xsl:for-each select="invoices/invoices_rec[
generate-id(.) = generate-id( key('invoiceid',
invoiceNum)[1])]"> ??
```

It's the grouping technique called Muenchian:

1. I defined a key (it works like a hashmap in C++), so I can look-up an invoices_rec by invoiceNum

```
<xsl:key name="invoiceid"
match="/database/invoices/invoices_rec"
use="invoiceNum"/>
```

2. I iterate on each invoices_rec but only considering the first one in the group (group by invoiceNum)

```
xsl:for-each select="invoices/invoices_rec[ generate-
id(.) = generate-id( key('invoiceid',
invoiceNum)[1])]">

invoices/invoices_rec[ ]
The expression inside the square brackets gets
evaluated for each invoices_rec

key('invoiceid', invoiceNum)[1]
```

These will return a list of invoices_rec given invoiceNum in the context. I'll take the first one:

generate-id
Returns a unique id for a given node that be used to check if two expressions are selecting the same node.

Here you can find several other techniques:

```
<p /><xsl:value-of select="contactName"/><br />
<xsl:value-of select="shipToAddress"/><br />
<xsl:value-of select="shipToCity"/><br />
<xsl:value-of select="shipToState"/><br />
<xsl:value-of select="shipToZip"/><br />

<!-- display NEW customer invoice details -->
<br/><p />INVOICE NUMBER: <xsl:value-of
select="invoiceNum"/>
<p />SALES DATE: <xsl:value-of
select="salesDate"/><br/><br/>

<!-- display new table headers -->
<table border="1">
<tr bgcolor="#9acd32">
<th>Product ID</th>
<th>Product Name</th>
<th>Product Description</th>
<th>Quantity</th>
<th>Unit Price</th>
<th>Extended Price</th>
</tr>
</table>

<!-- Store last invoiceNum -->
<xsl:for-each select="invoiceNum">
<xsl:variable name="last_invoice_number" select="."/>

</xsl:for-each>

</xsl:if>

<!-- display PRODUCT details in a table -->
<tr>
<td><xsl:value-of select="ProductID"/></td>
<td><xsl:value-of select="ProductName"/></td>
<td><xsl:value-of select="ProductDescription"/></td>
<td><xsl:value-of select="Quantity"/></td>
<td><xsl:value-of select="UnitPrice"/></td>
<td><xsl:value-of select="ExtendedPrice"/></td>
</tr>

</xsl:for-each>

<!-- Close last table -->
</table><br/><br/>

</body>
```

```
</html>

</xsl:template>
</xsl:stylesheet>
```

A: This is a basic grouping problem. Please use the attached solution to guide you in the right direction. And if you encounter this condition:

```
<xsl:for-each select="invoices/invoices_rec[
generate-id(.) = generate-id( key('invoiceid',
invoiceNum)[1])]"> ??
```

It's the grouping technique called Muenchian:

1. I defined a key (it works like a hashmap in C++), so I can look-up an invoices_rec by invoiceNum

```
<xsl:key name="invoiceid"
match="/database/invoices/invoices_rec"
use="invoiceNum"/>
```

2. I iterate on each invoices_rec but only considering the first one in the group (group by invoiceNum)

```
xsl:for-each select="invoices/invoices_rec[ generate-
id(.) = generate-id( key('invoiceid',
invoiceNum)[1])]">

invoices/invoices_rec[ ]
The expression inside the square brackets gets
evaluated for each invoices_rec

key('invoiceid', invoiceNum)[1]
```

These will return a list of invoices_rec given invoiceNum in the context. I'll take the first one:

generate-id
Returns a unique id for a given node that be used to check if two expressions are selecting the same node.

Here you can find several other techniques:

http://www.dpawson.co.uk/xsl/sect2/N4486.html

Question 69: Advanced Boolean Statements

I am trying to do the following:

```
count(/Rows/Row[Status = $status and
(Target_x0020_Release = 1.0 or Target_x0020_Release =
])
```

where the 'or' statement checks if there is nothing for Target_x0020_Release.

The desired outcome is that if Target_x0020_Release = 1.0 or if there is nothing in Target_x0020_Release, it will return true for the Status. I have tried a few things, but cannot get it.

A: Try the following:

```
count(/Rows/Row[Status = $status and
(Target_x0020_Release = '1.0' or Target_x0020_Release
= '')])
```

Question 70: XSLT, XALAN, Using XS[]

I am trying to terminate the XML conversion using xsl:message terminate = "yes"; the conversion is terminated, but I need to display a message indicating an error. But I can't find the message being displayed any where. Is there a way to output a message indicating the termination?

A: Yes, try doing this. <xsl:message terminate="yes">Stop here!</xsl:message> will stop the processor and send the "Stop here!" message to stderr.

In Stylus Studio that will be visible in the Output Window.

Question 71: Hiding Declarations in XSLT

I am using Stylus Studio 6 Enterprise Edition XSLT processor: Saxon 6.5.3. I am trying to hide certain elements in the output but am unable to do so:

```
<!-- Start: stylesheet.xsl --->
<xsl:stylesheet
xmlns:xsl="http://www.w3.org/1999/XSL/Transform"
version="1.0" xmlns:a="http://www.someurl.org/"
xmlns:xsi="http://www.w3.org/2001/XMLSchema-instance"
>

<xsl:output method="xml"/>

<elementRoot>
...
</elementRoot>

</xsl:stylesheet>
<!-- End: stylesheet.xsl -->

<!-- Output Obtained --->
<?xml version='1.0' ?>

<elementRoot xmlns:a="http://www.someurl.org/"
xmlns:xsi="http://www.w3.org/2001/XMLSchema-instance"
>
...
</elementRoot>


<!--output Desired -->

<elementRoot>
...
</elementRoot>
```

I do not want the XML declaration to show up in the output <?xml version='1.0' ?> should not be included. Also the elementRoot should not contain any namespace attributes.

How would I make this happen?

A: To remove namespace declarations from the output, you can use the attribute "exclude-result-prefixes" in the:

```
<xsl:stylesheet...> element; like:
<xsl:stylesheet .... exclude-result-prefixes="xsi a">
```

To remove the XML PI from the output, you can add omit-xml-declaration="yes" in your <xsl:output> element:

```
<xsl:output omit-xml-declaration="yes"/>
```

Question 72: Set Output Order

I need to have my output always in the same order. The XSL Stylesheet that follows, parses data from a "Multi-page" XML document. Each "Page" or node has a "@id" (W1S, W2S, W4S, W7S, WSA). Most of the documents that are parsed have nodes in this order, however, some have "page" or node W4S following "page" or node W7S, instead of node W2S. This causes a different sequence of elements, which, in turn, results in the output having a similarly different sequence. How can I modify the XSL Stylesheet to "force" the output to always appear in the same sequence, regardless of the sequence of the elements in the XML document being parsed?

A: You can do the following:

```
 <xsl:stylesheet
xmlns:xsl="http://www.w3.org/1999/XSL/Transform"
version="1.0">

<xsl:output method="text"/>

<xsl:template match="AppraisalForm">

<!-- Select specific Node or Form based on its id --
><xsl:if test="@id='W1S'">
File #<xsl:value-of select="field[@id='4']/value"/>|
Address <xsl:value-of
select="field[@id='1001']/value"/>|
City <xsl:value-of
```

```
select="field[@id='1002']/value"/>|
</xsl:if>

<!-- Select a different specific Node or form based
on its id --><xsl:if test="@id='W2S'">
Water <xsl:value-of
select="field[@id='14116']/value"/>|
Sewer <xsl:value-of
select="field[@id='14126']/value"/>|
Heat <xsl:value-of
select="field[@id='14127']/value"/>|
</xsl:if>

<!-- Select a different specific Node or form based
on its id --> <xsl:if test="@id='W4S'">
OAR SP <xsl:value-of
select="field[@id='60293']/value"/>|
GIM SP <xsl:value-of
select="field[@id='60291']/value"/>|
Sale Date <xsl:value-of
select="field[@id='60016']/value"/>|</xsl:if>

<!-- Select a different specific Node or form based
on its id --><xsl:if test="@id='W5S'">
Vac Percent <xsl:value-of
select="field[@id='80090']/value"/>|</xsl:if>

<!-- Select a different specific Node or form based
on its id --><xsl:if test="@id='W7S'">
Year <xsl:value-of
select="field[@id='150955']/value"/>|
Source <xsl:value-of
select="field[@id='152539']/value"/>|
Rental Inc <xsl:value-of
select="field[@id='150982']/value"/>|
Laundry <xsl:value-of
select="field[@id='150984']/value"/>|
</xsl:if>

<!-- Select a different specific Node or form based
on its id --><xsl:if test="@id='WSA'">
OAR Val <xsl:value-of
select="field[@id='97015']/value"/>|
GIM Val <xsl:value-of
select="field[@id='97000']/value"/>|
Value <xsl:value-of
select="field[@id='150615']/value"/>|
</xsl:if>
</xsl:template></xsl:stylesheet>
```

Question 73: Pass a Current Date

How do I pass a current date to XSL? I tried to pass param from C# and in XSL I have:

```
<xsl:param name="CurrentDate"></xsl:param>


<xsl:text>"Date Generated: </xsl:text>
<xsl:value-of select="$CurrentDate"/>
<xsl:text>",&#13;&#10;</xsl:text>
```

But it doesn't work. Did I miss something?

A: There is no "built-in" way to do that in XSLT 1.0; you can use an extension function from EXSLT to do that (http://www.exslt.org/date/index.html).

If you are using XSLT 2.0, then you can simply use the current-date() function. You can test the XSLT in Stylus Studio and experiment with parameters binding at the UI level; that will let you be sure that the XSLT itself is doing the right thing.

Question 74: Complicated XML Function

I have a problem converting the XML codes below into HTML. I know how to interpret the second and third line of XML by using XSL. However, if I wish to insert the first line of the XML file into HTML table (mo companydetail) right before the street and phone components, how will I modify my XSL?

```
<html>
<body>
<h2>company list></h2>
<tr bgcolor="#green">
<th align="center">street</th>
<th align="center">phone</th>
</tr>

<xsl:for-each select="/saved/mo">
<tr>
<td>
<xsl:value-of select="attribute[@name='street']"/>
</td>
<td>
<xsl:value-of select="attribute[@name=phone]"/>
</td>


</tr>
</xsl:for-each>
</table>
</body>
</html>

xml
----

<saved>

<mo companydetail="US,code=1011,company=AVAD"/>
<attribute name="street">121</attribute>
<attribute name="phone">3478665</attribute>


<mo companydetail="JAPAN,code=161,company=BPC"/>
```

```
<attribute name="street">15675</attribute>
<attribute name="phone">233534</attribute>

</saved>
```

A: You can make the following changes to correct your code formation:

```
<tr>
<td>
<xsl:value-of select="@companydetail"/>
</td>
<td>
<xsl:value-of select="attribute[@name='street']"/>
</td>
<td>
<xsl:value-of select="attribute[@name=phone]"/>
</td>
</tr>
```

Question 75: Problem Using Copy of "within"

I'm doing XML to XML conversion, I have some nodes which I don't need now, but I also do not want to lose the data in those tags. I tried copying them as comment in the resulting XML. The copy works fine, but when it's inside <xsl:comment> the copy does not occur properly. How can I overcome this? I need the same result, as it is when "copy of" is used. It must be commented though. What do I do?

A: You can do the following:

```
<xsl:text disable-output-escaping="yes">&lt;!--
</xsl:text>
<xsl:copy-of select="."/> <!-- or whatever else you
need to select -->
<xsl:text disable-output-escaping="yes">--
&gt;</xsl:text>
```

Question 76: Value of Select Doubt

I have one of the attributes in XML where it is too long to put into a table. I wish to do some filtering before putting it into the HTML table.

```
<attribute name="address">28 thomson
road,poscode=75500</attribute>
```

Which part of my code (below) should be modified in order to select only poscode value?

```
<xsl:value-of select="attribute[@name='address']"/>
```

A: You could do it this way:

```
<xsl:value-of select="attribute[@name='address' and
contains(.,'poscode=75500']"/>
```

Or you can do more sophisticated checks using other XPath functions to manipulate strings. And if you want to display the poscode value only, you can do something like:

```
<xsl:value-of select="substring-
after(attribute[@name='address'],'poscode=')"/>
```

Question 77: XSLT and File List

I'm trying to output an HTML or XML file including a list of XML files (path and file name) within a directory. I have three XML files:

```
C:\temp\1.xml
C:\temp\2.xml
C:\temp\3.xml
```

My XSL has to get the path in the file name of those XML files and output a file like this:

```
<files>
<file>C:\temp\1.xml</file>
<file>C:\temp\2.xml</file>
<file>C:\temp\3.xml</file>
</files>
```

Is this possible? If so, how can I make it work? Is it possible for a new XML file (..\4.xml) to be saved in this directory?

A: If you are asking if you can access an XML file (other than the default input) from XSLT, you can do that using the document() function, using any suitable XPath expression as argument.

There is no native way to make XSLT read the content of a folder. You will need to create an extension function (Java or different scripting language depending on the target processor) to do that.

Question 78: XSLT 2.0 Calendar

I'd like to generate a simple calendar using XSLT 2.0. Is there any way to know:

1. How many days are there in a given month?
2. How to add a duration to a given date (e.g., add a day to '2006-03-31' to produce '2006-04-01')?

There appears to be lots of new date formatting, extraction and duration functions in the XSLT 2.0 spec, but I can't find any that can achieve the above. I'm using SS 2006 Enterprise R2 with Saxon 8.7. How can I accomplish objectives 1 and 2?

A: Answers are provided below according to how they were asked.

1. With this, you could use a sequence of 12 items and index that on the required month handling exceptions for leap years. Or you can rely on XPath date functions:

```
declare function local:getDaysInMonth($date as
xs:date) as xs:integer
{
let $nextMonth := month-from-date($date)+1
return
if($nextMonth = 13) then 31
else
day-from-date(xs:date( concat(year-from-
date($date),'-',if ($nextMonth>9) then $nextMonth
else concat('0',$nextMonth),'-','01')) -
xdt:dayTimeDuration('P1D'))
};
```

Then you can call:
`local:getDaysInMonth('2006-04-01')`

2. `xs:date('2006-04-30')+xdt:dayTimeDuration('P1D')`

Question 79: XSL Looping

I want to loop through a string. I have a variable with 15 characters in length.

```
var1 = ab-defghijklmno
```

And I want to output it in a table:

```
<table>
<tr>
<td>a</td>
<td>b</td>
<td bgcolor="black"> </td>
<td>e</td>
etc.
```

I want it to loop through the string, if it comes across a '-' character write a different td output. Sounds simple, but I cannot do it. How can I accomplish this?

A: The following may be useful:

```
<xsl:template match="/">
<table>
<tr>
<xsl:call-template name="explodeString">
<xsl:with-param name="txt" select="'ab-defg'"/>
</xsl:call-template>
</tr>
</table>
</xsl:template>

<xsl:template name="explodeString">
<xsl:param name="txt"/>
<xsl:param name="pos" select="1"/>

<xsl:choose>
<xsl:when test="substring($txt, $pos, 1) = '-'">
<td>something special</td>
</xsl:when>
<xsl:otherwise>
<td>
<xsl:value-of select="substring($txt, $pos, 1)"/>
</td>
</xsl:otherwise>
```

```
</xsl:choose>
<xsl:if test="$pos &lt; string-length($txt)">
<xsl:call-template name="explodeString">
<xsl:with-param name="txt" select="$txt"/>
<xsl:with-param name="pos" select="$pos+1"/>
</xsl:call-template>
</xsl:if>
</xsl:template>
```

Question 80: Namespace Doesn't Contain Any Functions

I am trying to run a sample .XSL against some simple .XML. The XSL includes use of the node set function which I think is an extension: (xalan:nodeset). I get the following errors:

```
Namespace 'http://xml.apache.org/xalan' does not
contain any functions
```

How do I sort through this error?

A: Choose XalanJ as your XSLT processor in XSLT > Scenario > Processor tab; then run the Stylus Studio.

Question 81: Node-set - Arrays in XSLT

I want to parse an XML doc and store the results in a Data Structure so I can later iterate over to an array. I read that XSLT doesn't support Arrays. However, there's a node-set which will let me do this looping over a subset of the xml stored in the node-set structure. Is there an example that I could study or is there any other Data Structures that would be suitable for this?

A: If you use the "books.xml" file shipped as part of the example Stylus Studio project, you can, as an example, do something like this:

```
<xsl:template match="/">
<!-- collect all books satisfying some condition in a
variable -->
<xsl:variable name="myBooks">
<xsl:for-each select="books/book[@bookid &lt; 3]">
<xsl:copy-of select="."/>
</xsl:for-each>
</xsl:variable>

<!-- output the title of the first book referenced by
the variable -->
<firstOne>
<xsl:value-of select="$myBooks[1]/book/title"/>
</firstOne>
</xsl:template>
```

You can practice this to perfection. Just give it time.

Question 82: Including FO Document in Output

I am using XSLT to transform CSV files into FO tables (see attached for sample). These works fine when I cut and paste the generated FO code into the XSL code window. However, I need to include the FO files during processing.

I have tried using XSL:VALUE-OF SELECT DOCUMENT - this ignores the FO commands and simply outputs the text from the cells unformatted. I have tried using UNPARSED-TEXT and it outputs the complete FO code as a string. I just need to pass the FO code to be included in the final FO output file (much like including an SVG file). How can I successfully implement this?

A: To include "fo document" in output, do this:

```
<xsl:copy-of select="document(...
```

Question 83: Checkbox Query Checked State

I have added a checkbox to my XSLT and want to check its state in a "choose conditional". How is this done?

A: Just do the following:

```
<input type="checkbox">
<xsl:choose>
<xsl:when test="someXPathCondition">
<xsl:attribute name="checked"/>
</xsl:when>
</xsl:choose>
</input>
```

Question 84: Formatting Whole Number to Percentages

I have a whole number in my XML document (41) for example, and need it to display it as 41.0%. I have tried formatting as: 0.0% and several methods, but I am getting 4100.00% instead. How can I do this right?

A: Use the following:

```
<xsl:value-of select="format-
number(satisfied,'#.0')"/>%
```

Question 85: Hyperlink Creation Problem

I'm having trouble outputting an XML cross-reference to HTML.

The XML is:

```
<para>For more information see <link
format = "Heading on page x"
srcfile =
"CompletePubFlowDevPage2.xml#BABJEADD"/>.</para>
```

I'm able to output an active hyperlink using this rule:

```
<xsl:template match="link">
<a href="{@srcfile}">
<xsl:value-of select="@format"/>
```

However, I don't want the value of the format attribute to be the link text. Instead, I want the text in the link element. When I replace "@format" with "link" I get this:

```
<a href="CompletePubFlowDevPage2.xml#BABJEADD"></a>
```

which doesn't give me a link to click on. How can I do this?

A: If your XML fragment is:

```
<para>For more information see <link
format = "Heading on page x"
srcfile =
"CompletePubFlowDevPage2.xml#BABJEADD"/>.</para>
```

Then the <link> element has no text. In your XML fragment the only element that has text associated is <para>. If that's what you are trying to output from inside the template matching <link>, you will have to do <xsl:value-of select=".."/>.

Question 86: Multiple Entries for 1 Heading

I am working with the attached XML and I want to list all of the projects (Title) that a person is working on. Now, it just lists one of them. I tried modifying a template used for the priority averaging piece, but I do not think that it will work.

A: Instead of doing <xsl:value-of select="Title"/> for the project cell (you don't even have a Title element in the source XML...), you can try something like this:

```
<ul>
<xsl:for-each select="//Row[substring-
after(Assigned_x0020_To,'#') = $name]">
<li>
<xsl:value-of select="_ListTitle"/>
</li>
</xsl:for-each>
</ul>
```

(assuming _ListTitle is the project name); or you can create a nested table, whatever works best for the presentation style you are looking for.

Question 87: Converting a Number to String

I have this:

```
<xsl:when test="contains(string(sum(//Row[substring-
after(Assigned_x0020_To,'#') =
$name]/Percent_x0020_Bandwidth * 100)),'.')">
<td>
<center>
<xsl:value-of select="substring-
before(sum(//Row[substring-
after(Assigned_x0020_To,'#') =
$name]/Percent_x0020_Bandwidth) * 100,'.')"/> %
</center>
</td>
</xsl:when>
```

However, it is not functioning. I would like to check if there is a decimal point in the number. If there is, then I would like to output the numbers before the decimal point. Is there an easier way that could make this functional?

A: Use the following: “format-number(<number>, '#')”.

Question 88: Pass Multiple Values to XSL

I use ASP (vbscript), XML, and XSLT to generate HTML output to browsers. In this page, I need to list files in a directory on the server. If this was an ASP (classic) page I'd simply do this using FileSystemObject, but how do I go about listing the files in XSLT? I use xsl:addParameter often to pass values to my XSL pages, but in this case where the number of filenames are unknown and I cannot see that this is an option. Is there any other option for me?

A: Yes, there is. Use a parameter that is a result tree fragment listing all the entries you need to access from the XSLT.

Question 89: Exemplar XSLT Transformations

I would like to use Stylus Studio to run the following transformation:

```
<?xml version='1.0'?>
<person xsl:version="1.0"
xmlns:xsl="http://www.w3.org/1999/XSL/Transform">
<name2><xsl:value-of
select="concat(/muppets/muppet/surname, ' ',
/muppets/muppet/name)" /></name2>
<description><xsl:value-of
select="/muppets/muppet/description"/></description>
</person>
```

On the following document:

```
<?xml version="1.0"?>
<muppets>
<muppet>
<surname/>
<name>Kermit</name>
<description>The most well-known
Muppet!</description>
<rating>high</rating>
</muppet>
<muppet>
<surname/>
<name>Gonzo</name>
<description>A unique blue Muppet!</description>
<rating>medium</rating>
</muppet>
<muppet>
<surname>Ms.</surname>
<name>Piggy</name>
<description>An annoying female pig.</description>
<rating>low</rating>
</muppet>
</muppets>
```

When I try to run the transformation via the "Scenario" view, it complains that I haven't started with a <stylesheet> or <transform> element. Does this mean I can't use the exemplar-style method of writing transforms in Stylus Studio, or is there some step I'm missing?

A: You are using one of the simplified stylesheet syntaxes described in the XSLT Recommendation, Section 2.3. As mentioned in the Stylus Studio Release Notes, this is not supported by the built-in XSLT processor. However, your XSLT will run if you use the XalanJ or Saxon processors.

You can also change the processor on the Processor tab of the Scenario Properties dialog box. Click XSLT > Scenario Properties, or click the [...] button to the right of the Scenario drop-down list in the XSLT Editor to display it.

Question 90: Convert RTF to XML/XSLT

I'm trying to convert a RTF file to XML and it doesn't seem to work.

First, I used WordPad to create a file with certain settings like bigger font and highlighted it with color. I saved it as an RTF file. Then I converted it to an RTF document into an XML format using the Stylus Studio converters (when opening the RTF file, click the "Convert to XML" button in the Open File dialog, and then choose the RTF converter) which open the file using the Convert To XML. But there is no way for me to see the same setting as it supposed to have with this RTF file.

What should I do in order to see the exact same format setting? Is there any configuration or setting that needs to be done?

A: The XML converters will translate the RTF format into an XML format, including the formatting information. But you shouldn't expect to see the formatting information rendered as the text *format*; you will see the formatting information returned as part of the XML information in which the RTF is encoded.

For example, if you try to write a few words in WordPad, save the result and open it specifying to convert it to XML and then choosing the RTF converter, you will get this XML document:

```
<rtf value="1">
<ansi/>
<ansicpg value="1252"/>
<deff value="0"/>
<deflang value="1033"/>
<fonttbl>
<f value="0">
<fswiss/>
<fcharset value="0"/>Arial;</f>
</fonttbl>
<generator ignorable="yes">Msftedit
5.41.15.1507;</generator>
<viewkind value="4"/>
<uc value="1"/>
<pard/>
<f value="0"/>
<fs value="20"/>I am a test!<par/></rtf>
```

Note the "I am a test" string at the bottom; that's what I typed. Now, go back to WordPad, and make "test" bold; refresh the document in Stylus Studio and you will get this:

```
<?xml version="1.0" encoding="utf-8"?>
<rtf value="1">
<ansi/>
<ansicpg value="1252"/>
<deff value="0"/>
<deflang value="1033"/>
<fonttbl>
<f value="0">
<fswiss/>
<fcharset value="0"/>Arial;</f>
</fonttbl>
<generator ignorable="yes">Msftedit
5.41.15.1507;</generator>
<viewkind value="4"/>
<uc value="1"/>
<pard/>
<f value="0"/>
<fs value="20"/>I am a <b/> test<b value="0"/> !
<par/></rtf>
```

Note that the "test" block is now marked as being bold. Other formatting instructions will be formatted in a similar way.

The XML conversion of RTF preserves the formatting information; but the raw XML itself is not a presentation language; it won't "render" the formatting information as you would see it. But once the RTF is available as XML you can use it to carry one additional computation, or even to transform the document in some different presentational language (like HTML).

Question 91: No Average Function in Stylus

I have a footer summing up two different columns "Num Surveyed", and Num Responses" which works fine. However, in the last column, which contains the Average of column 1 and column 2, I do not need a total, but an average of that column "Response Rate". I get an error message in WYSIWYG that there is no average function. Is there a way I can do the math manually and divide the column two by column 1?

I have tried the "div" operator with no success.

A: The following should work:

```
<xsl:value-of select="format-number( sum(
datasettablename/response_rate ) div
count(datasettablename/response_rate), '0.0%')" />
```

Question 92: Suppressing Data on Following Rows

I have an XML file with elements such as: year, month, Number surveyed, number responses, and response rate. There are five (5) columns for a table. How can I print the year only?

A: You can change the line that outputs your year into:

```
<xsl:choose>
<xsl:when test="preceding-
sibling::datasettablename[1]/out_year =
out_year">&quot;</xsl:when>
<xsl:otherwise>
<xsl:value-of select="out_year"/>
</xsl:otherwise>
</xsl:choose>
```

Question 93: Exceeding Recursive Limit Using SAXON Processor

I have developed a Version 2 xslt transformation stylesheet. I keep on hitting the error "java.lang.RuntimeException: Maximum Recursion Depth exceeded". I already have the maximum setting of 500 selected in the XSLT Settings window. I have seen an example which increases the recursion limit by creating a registry entry at HCU\software\ExcelonCorporation\StylusStudio\PluginSettings called XSLTEditor: Option: RecursionLevel (REG_SZ type) and setting to 10000 but this has had no effect in my case. I think this may apply only to the internal processor.

How can I increase the recursion level for the Saxon processor above the 500 limit of the user-interface?

A: That registry key was good back in the old days, but Stylus Studio doesn't belong to eXcelon Corporation. It is now part of Data Direct, so we've renamed the key.

If you were using 2006 Enterprise, you can use this:

```
Windows Registry Editor Version 5.00:

[HKEY_CURRENT_USER\Software\Stylus Studio\XML
Enterprise Edition 2006\Plugin Settings]
"XSLT Editor: Option: RecursionLevel"=dword:00002710
```

Question 94: XSL Problem

Recently I had a problem converting XML to HTML. Here is the table that I wish to appear in HTML:

```
name sex code job
steven male 1 accountant
richard male 2 engineer
daniel male 3 scientist
```

I can't convert to HTML as what I wanted.xml code as below:

```
<?xml version="1.0" encoding="UTF-8"?>
<?xml-stylesheet type="text/xsl" href="inter2.xsl"?>
<saved>
<mo>
<attribute name="job">accountant</attribute>
<attribute name="sex">male</attribute>
<attribute name="code">1</attribute>
<attribute name="name">steven</attribute>
</mo>
<mo>
<attribute name="job">engineer</attribute>
<attribute name="sex">male</attribute>
<attribute name="code">2</attribute>
<attribute name="name">richard</attribute>
</mo>
<mo>
<attribute name="job">scientist</attribute>
<attribute name="sex">male</attribute>
<attribute name="code">3</attribute>
<attribute name="name">daniel</attribute>
</mo>
</saved>
```

This is my XSL:

```
<?xml version="1.0" encoding="ISO-8859-1"?>
<!-- Edited with XML Spy v4.2 -->
<xsl:stylesheet version="1.0"
xmlns:xsl="http://www.w3.org/1999/XSL/Transform">
<xsl:output method='html' version='1.0'
encoding='UTF-8' indent='yes'/>
<xsl:template match="saved">
<html>
<body>
<h2>FIRST TRIAL</h2>
<table border="2">
<tr bgcolor="#black">
<th align="center">job</th>
<th align="center">sex</th>
<th align="center">code</th>
<th align="center">name</th>
</tr>
<xsl:for-each select="mo/attribute">
<tr>
<td><xsl:value-of select="."/></td>
<td><xsl:value-of select="."/></td>
<td><xsl:value-of select="."/></td>
<td><xsl:value-of select="."/></td>
</tr>
</xsl:for-each>
</table>
</body>
</html>
</xsl:template>
</xsl:stylesheet>
```

What is my error on the XSL code? How do I correct this?

A: You can try something like the following:

```
<?xml version="1.0" encoding="ISO-8859-1"?>
<!-- Edited with Stylus Studio 2006 Enterprise
Edition -->
<xsl:stylesheet version="1.0"
xmlns:xsl="http://www.w3.org/1999/XSL/Transform">
<xsl:output method="html" version="1.0"
encoding="UTF-8" indent="yes"/>
<xsl:template match="saved">
<html>
<body>
<h2>FIRST TRIAL</h2>
```

```
<table border="2">
<tr bgcolor="#black">
<th align="center">job</th>
<th align="center">sex</th>
<th align="center">code</th>
<th align="center">name</th>
</tr>
<xsl:for-each select="/saved/mo">
<tr>
<td>
<xsl:value-of select="attribute[@name='job']"/>
</td>
<td>
<xsl:value-of select="attribute[@name='sex']"/>
</td>
<td>
<xsl:value-of select="attribute[@name='code']"/>
</td>
<td>
<xsl:value-of select="attribute[@name='name']"/>
</td>
</tr>
</xsl:for-each>
</table>
</body>
</html>
</xsl:template>
</xsl:stylesheet>
```

Question 95: Summation in XSLT

How do I handle the following scenario?

```
 Source XML <?xml version="1.0" encoding="UTF-8" ?>
<root>< <del> <value> <p1>10</p1> <p2>5</p2> </value>
<value> <p1>10</p1> <p2>5</p2> </value> <value>
<p1>10</p1> <p2>15</p2> </value> </del> </root>
Target XML <?xml version="1.0" encoding="UTF-8" ?>
<root> <del> <value>35</value> </del> </root>
```

I am trying to be able to compare the value <p1> and <p2> and pick up the greater of the 2 and sum it up. So in our above example it becomes 10 + 10 + 15 = 35. How can this be achieved using XSLT 1.0?

A: There are ways to do this in a much simpler way using XSLT 2.0. You can also use XSLT 1.0. The following should do something similar to what you are looking for:

```
<?xml version="1.0"?>
<xsl:stylesheet version="1.0"
xmlns:xsl="http://www.w3.org/1999/XSL/Transform">
<xsl:template match="/">
<root>
<del>
<value>
<xsl:apply-templates select="/root/del/value[1]"/>
</value>
</del>
</root>
</xsl:template>
<xsl:template match="value">
<xsl:param name="curSum" select="0"/>
<xsl:variable name="aValue">
<xsl:choose>
<xsl:when test="p1 &gt; p2">
<xsl:value-of select="p1"/>
</xsl:when>
<xsl:otherwise>
<xsl:value-of select="p2"/>
</xsl:otherwise>
</xsl:choose>
</xsl:variable>
<xsl:choose>
```

```
<xsl:when test="following-sibling::value[1]">
<xsl:apply-templates select="following-
sibling::value[1]">
<xsl:with-param name="curSum"
select="$curSum+$aValue"/>
</xsl:apply-templates>
</xsl:when>
<xsl:otherwise>
<xsl:value-of select="$curSum+$aValue"/>
</xsl:otherwise>
</xsl:choose>
</xsl:template>
</xsl:stylesheet>
```

Question 96: Double Grouping

I need to transform the following XML file into batches by ship method and then into groups of 3.

```
<DetailList>
<details>
<name>Bob</name>
<address>Your House</address>
<merchant>Home Depot</merchant>
<productValue>50.00</productValue>
<shipMethod>RUSH</shipMethod>
</details>
<details>
<name>Jim</name>
<address>Your House</address>
<merchant>Home Depot</merchant>
<productValue>50.00</productValue>
<shipMethod>UPS</shipMethod>
</details>
......etc.
</DetailList>
```

I can group it by ship method with:

```
<xsl:template match="/DetailList">
<Batches>
<xsl:for-each-group select="details" group-
by="shipMethod">
<Batch id="{current-grouping-key()}">
```

```
<xsl:apply-templates select="current-group()"/>
</Batch>
</xsl:for-each-group>
</Batches>
</xsl:template>

<xsl:template match="*">
<xsl:copy-of select="."/>
</xsl:template>
```

And I can also group into groups of 3 with:

```
<xsl:param name="max" select="3"/>

<xsl:template match="/ALGGiftCard" name="number">
<BatchList>
<xsl:for-each select="details[position() mod $max =
1]">
<Batch>
<xsl:for-each select=". | following-
sibling::details[position() &lt; $max]">
<xsl:call-template name="copyAll"/>
</xsl:for-each>
</Batch>
</xsl:for-each>
</BatchList>
</xsl:template>

<xsl:template name="copyAll" match="*">
<xsl:copy-of select="."/>
</xsl:template>
```

But I am at a lost when trying to combine them together. The resulting XML file needs to look something like:

```
<Batch id="RUSH_1">
<details>
<name>Bob</name>
<address>Your House</address>
<merchant>Home Depot</merchant>
<productValue>50.00</productValue>
<shipMethod>RUSH</shipMethod>
</details>
<details>
<name>Larry</name>
<address>Your House</address>
<merchant>Lowes</merchant>
<productValue>20.00</productValue>
```

```
<shipMethod>RUSH</shipMethod>
</details>
<details>
<name>Pappy</name>
<address>Your House</address>
<merchant>KMart</merchant>
<productValue>150,000.00</productValue>
<shipMethod>RUSH</shipMethod>
</details>
</Batch>
<Batch id="RUSH_2">
<details>
<name>Jim</name>
<address>Your House</address>
<merchant>Home Depot</merchant>
<productValue>50.00</productValue>
<shipMethod>RUSH</shipMethod>
</details>
<details>
<name>Ken</name>
<address>Your House</address>
<merchant>Lowes</merchant>
<productValue>20.00</productValue>
<shipMethod>RUSH</shipMethod>
</details>
<details>
<name>Jose</name>
<address>Your House</address>
<merchant>KMart</merchant>
<productValue>150,000.00</productValue>
<shipMethod>RUSH</shipMethod>
</details>
</Batch>
```

How can I make this work?

A: This may help:

```
<xsl:stylesheet version="1.0"
xmlns:xsl="http://www.w3.org/1999/XSL/Transform">
<xsl:param name="max" select="3"/>
<xsl:key name="group" match="details"
use="shipMethod"/>
<xsl:template match="/">
<AllBatches>
<xsl:for-each select="//details[generate-id() =
generate-id(key('group', shipMethod)[1])]">
<xsl:variable name="shipMethod" select="shipMethod"/>
```

```
<Group>
<xsl:attribute name="shipMethod">
<xsl:value-of select="$shipMethod"/>
</xsl:attribute>
<xsl:for-each select="//details[shipMethod =
$shipMethod and count(preceding-sibling::*[shipMethod
= $shipMethod]) mod $max = 0]">
<Batch>
<xsl:attribute name="id">
<xsl:value-of select="position()"/>
</xsl:attribute>
<xsl:variable name="listPosition"
select="count(preceding-sibling::*[shipMethod =
$shipMethod])"/>
<xsl:for-each select="//details[shipMethod =
$shipMethod]">
<xsl:if test="position() &gt; $listPosition and
position() &lt;= $listPosition + $max">
<xsl:copy-of select="."/>
</xsl:if>
</xsl:for-each>
</Batch>
</xsl:for-each>
</Group>
</xsl:for-each>
</AllBatches>
</xsl:template>
</xsl:stylesheet>
```

Question 97: Path Problem

With this input:

```
<doc>
<bs>
<b><c>A</c><d>AAA</d></b>
<b><c>B</c><d>BBB</d></b>
<b><c>C</c><d>CCC</d></b>
<b><c>D</c><d>DDD</d></b>
</bs>
<body>
<x>A</x>
<x>D</x>
</body>
</doc>
```

I want to expand the codes (A, D) to their values in the BS table. (AAA, DDD). This template works:

```
<xsl:template match="x">
<xsl:variable name="x">
<xsl:value-of select="."/>
</xsl:variable>
<xsl:value-of select="/doc/bs/b[c=$x]/d)"/>
</xsl:template>
```

But this does not perform as attempted:

```
<xsl:template match="x">
<xsl:value-of select="/doc/bs/b[c=.]/d)"/>
</xsl:template>
```

How do I correct this?

A: When you create a predicate inside brackets (b[c=$x], for example), you are setting a new input context set to the current node being examined by the predicate. The variable you set in your first XSLT sample is what allows you to compare a node with the input context of the template.

The reason your second XSLT doesn't work is that when the evaluation reaches the predicate (b[c=.]), the context node points to a "b" node. In order to reach the "x" node, you either need to use the current() function (like [c=current()], for example), or store the value of "." as a variable and use it later (as you did in your first XSLT).

Question 98: Elements Containing Attributes of a Specific Value

I have an XML file structured as follows:

```
<level1 attribute1>
<level2>
<level3 attribute1 />
</level2>
<level2>
<level3 attribute1 />
</level2>
<level1>
```

I want to be able to display a table that only shows the level1 attribute 1 if level3 attribute1 is equal to a certain value.

In real world terms I want to be able to display only those <file> elements whose <violation> element contains a "priority" attribute of a particular value. I can get the XSLT to display all <file> elements showing only the <violation> elements whose priority is of a particular value. However, it still shows every <file> regardless of whether it contains a <violation> whose priority is the one I'm trying to match. How do I accomplish my objectives?

A: You can change:

```
<xsl:for-each select="file">
```

into:

```
<xsl:for-each select="file[violation/@priority=2]">
```

Question 99: Adding a New Tag

I encountered trouble using XSL with a new tag. For example, I have:

```
<Rec><No>1</NO></Rec>
<Rec><No>2</NO></Rec>
<Rec><No>3</NO></Rec>
```

How to change as

```
<new data>
<Rec><No>1</NO></Rec>
<Rec><No>2</NO></Rec>
<Rec><No>3</NO></Rec>
</new data>
```

How do I make this work?

A: Use this:

```
<NewData>
<xsl:for-each select="//Rec">
<xsl:copy-of select="."/>
</xsl:for-each>
</NewData>
```

Question 100: XSLT of XSD

I have an XSD:

```
<?xml version="1.0" encoding="UTF-8"?>
<?xml-stylesheet type="text/xsl" href="test.xsl"?>
<xs:schema
xmlns:xs="http://www.w3.org/2001/XMLSchema"
elementFormDefault="qualified"
attributeFormDefault="unqualified">
<xs:simpleType name="deviceType">
<xs:restriction base="xs:string">
<xs:enumeration value="Test1"/>
<xs:enumeration value="Test2"/>
<xs:enumeration value="Test3"/>
<xs:enumeration value="Test4"/>
<xs:enumeration value="Test5"/>
</xs:restriction>
</xs:simpleType>
</xs:schema>
```

I would like to do an XSLT so that my output looks like:

```
<?xml version="1.0" encoding="UTF-8"?>
<output name="Test details">
<entry name="Test1" value="Test1"/>
<entry name="Test2" value="Test2"/>
<entry name="Test3" value="Test3"/>
<entry name="Test4" value="Test4"/>
<entry name="Test5" value="Test5"/>
</output>
```

I tried this xslt(test.xsl) but I get an empty XML file.

```
<?xml version="1.0" encoding="ISO-8859-1"?>
<xsl:stylesheet version="1.0"
xmlns:xsl="http://www.w3.org/1999/XSL/Transform">
<xsl:template match="deviceType">
<output name="Test details">
<xsl:for-each
select="xs:schema/xs:simpleType/restriction/xs:enumer
ation">
<entry>
<name><xsl:value-of select="@value"/></name>
<value><xsl:value-of select="@value"/></value>
</entry>
</xsl:for-each>
```

```
</output>
</xsl:template>
</xsl:stylesheet>
```

Can anyone help?

A: You were correct to use namespaces and for-each loops, but you forgot to first define the XS element before using it. This and some other errors in your code sample should be corrected in the following snippet:

```
<xsl:template match="/"
xmlns:xs="http://www.w3.org/2001/XMLSchema">
<output name="Test details">
<xsl:for-each
select="xs:schema/xs:simpleType/xs:restriction/xs:enu
meration">
<entry>
<name>
<xsl:value-of select="@value"/>
</name>
<value>
<xsl:value-of select="@value"/>
</value>
</entry>
</xsl:for-each>
</output>
</xsl:template>
```

Also, when you have time, check out Mulberry Tech's XSLT forum. It's a great resource for questions about XSLT usage:

http://www.mulberrytech.com/xsl/xsl-list/

Question 101: Nested Element Trouble in XSL

I am running into problems with XSL where I want to be able to nest XML elements in my schema like this:

```
<xs:element name="text">
 <xs:complexType mixed="true">
  <xs:all minOccurs="0">
   <xs:element name="bold" type="xs:string"
minOccurs="0"/>
  </xs:all>
 </xs:complexType>
</xs:element>
```

For example:

```
<text>this is a sample text with a <bold>bold</bold>
word in it</text>
```

I don't seem to getting my XSL right. At the moment I tried a few things, the most effective being:

```
<xsl:when test="text/bold">
  <xsl:value-of select="text"></xsl:value-
of><b><xsl:value-of select="text/bold"></xsl:value-
of></b>
</xsl:when>
```

which results in:

```
"This is a sample text with a bold word in it bold."
```

I am totally at a loss at this moment. All the other hard things (like automatic numbering, index building, image lists, in-document linking, etc.) I had to do I finished well ahead of time. But this tiny thing I can't seem to finish. What else should I do?

A: Look at this as an example.

I ran this XSL:

```
<xsl:template match="/">
  <xsl:apply-templates/>
```

```
</xsl:template>

<xsl:template match="*"/>

<xsl:template match="root">
  <xsl:apply-templates/>
</xsl:template>

<xsl:template match="text">
  <some-html-tags>
  <xsl:apply-templates/>
  </some-html-tags>
</xsl:template>

<xsl:template match="bold">
  <b><xsl:apply-templates/></b>
</xsl:template>
```

On this XML:

```
<root>
  <text>This is a <bold>bold</bold> word.</text>
  <something-else>this should not be
parsed</something-else>
  <text>And <bold>this</bold> is too</text>
  <something-else>this should not be
parsed</something-else>
  <text>But this is not</text>
</root>
```

And it worked OK. Or try replacing:

```
<xsl:template match="text">
  <some-html-tags>
  <xsl:apply-templates/>
  </some-html-tags>
</xsl:template>

<xsl:template match="bold">
  <b><xsl:apply-templates/></b>
</xsl:template>
```

With:

```
<xsl:template match="bold">
  <b><xsl:apply-templates/></b>
</xsl:template>
```

```
<xsl:template match="text">
  <some-html-tags>
  <xsl:apply-templates/>
  </some-html-tags>
</xsl:template>
```

<xsl:template-match> is an essential element in XSL.

Question 102: XSLT Grouping

I am trying to output a "select" field from the sample XML below:

```
<tree>
    <option>Ducks</option>
    <option>Cows</option>
    <option>Sheep</option>
    <option>Sheep</option>
    <option>Ducks</option>
    <option>Cows</option>
    <option>Cows</option>
</tree>
```

I need to group the option values to produce the sample HTML:

```
<select name="animals">
    <option>Cows</option>
    <option>Ducks</option>
    <option>Sheep</option>
</select>
```

Can anyone help me with the grouping in XSLT?

A: Try this:

```
<?xml version="1.0" encoding="ISO-8859-1"
standalone="yes"?>
<xsl:stylesheet
xmlns:xsl="http://www.w3.org/1999/XSL/Transform";
version="1.0">
<xsl:output method="html" indent="yes" encoding="iso-
8859-1" omit-xml-declaration="yes"/>

    <xsl:template match="/tree">

        <HTML>
```

```
            <BODY>
                <TABLE>
                    <TR>
                        <TD>
                            <SELECT>
                                <xsl:for-each
select="option">
                                    <xsl:variable
name="pre-option">
                                        <xsl:for-each
select="preceding-sibling::*">
                                            <xsl:valu
e-of select="concat(.,',')"/>
                                        </xsl:for-
each>
                                    </xsl:variable>
                                    <xsl:if
test="not(contains($pre-option, . ))">
                                        <OPTION>
                                            <xsl:valu
e-of select="."/>
                                        </OPTION>
                                    </xsl:if>
                                </xsl:for-each>
                            </SELECT>
                        </TD>
                    </TR>
                </TABLE>
            </BODY>
        </HTML>
    </xsl:template>

</xsl:stylesheet>
```

Question 103: XSL and Preceding-Sibling Question

I am trying to create XSL to transform such an XML structure in HTML:

```
<FACT>
  <TYPDET typ='N'>
    <DCO cta='123' dde='1'/>
    <DCO cta='456' dde='1'/>
    <DCO cta='456' dde='2'/>
    <DCO cta='789' dde='1'/>
  </TYPDET>
  <TYPDET typ='T'>
    <DCO cta='123' dde='2'/>
    <DCO cta='456' dde='1'/>
    <DCO cta='456' dde='3'/>
    <DCO cta='789' dde='1'/>
  </TYPDET>
</FACT>
```

I am in a template based on the DCO tag. If the value of TYPDET changes, I want to write a title like: 'Part' + type attribute. My problem is that I don't do the correct test on TYPDET when I am in my DCO template. I have tried :

```
<xsl:when test="../preceding-
sibling::TYPDET[position()=1]/@typ!=../@typ">
```

But it writes a title for each line of the second typdet paragraph. I have tried other things I don't remember, but I never get what I want. How can I do it right?

A: Try it at first with value-of and look at what you're getting:

```
<xsl:value-of select="../preceding-
sibling::TYPDET[1]/@typ/>
<xsl:value-of select="../@typ"/>
```

After that compare it in a test of xsl:when.

Question 104: Grouping with XSLT

I would like to be able to group my data, but I am not sure on the best way to go about this. Here is the structure before and what I would like to see afterwards.

Before:

```
<NewRoot>
   <General>
     <field1>x</field1>
     <field2>y</field2>
     <field3>z</field3>
   <General>
<NewRoot>
```

After:

```
<NewRoot>
   <General>
       <!---For Each Distinct Field1-->
       <field1>
           <field2>y</field2>
           <field3>z</field3>
       </field1>
    </General>
</NewRoot>
```

Can anyone point me in the right direction or does anyone know of some good articles to read?

A: You can do this:

```
 <?xml version='1.0'?>
  <xsl:stylesheet
xmlns:xsl="http://www.w3.org/1999/XSL/Transform";
version="1.0">
  <xsl:output method="html" />

    <xsl:variable name="Table" select="//Table" />

    <!--  Template for root rule -->
    <xsl:template match="/">
    <xsl:apply-templates />
    </xsl:template>
```

```
    <xsl:template match="NewDataSet">


    <xsl:for-each select="$Table">

    <!--  Sort Primary key ascending order -->
    <xsl:sort select="Field1" order="ascending" />

    <xsl:variable name="Field1" select="Field1" />
            <xsl:if test="generate-id(.)=generate-
id($Table[Field1=$Field1])">

            <!--  Display the table header -->
            <h5>
                <xsl:value-of select="Field1" />
            </h5>

            <!-- Display all node headers-->
            <table class="bordertext" cellSpacing="0"
cellPadding="1"  border="0" >
                <tr>
                    <th width="50">Detail Link</th>
                    <th width="75">Field 2</th>
                    <th width="100">Field 3</th>
                    <th width="75">Field 4</th>
                    <th width="150">Field 5</th>
                    <th width="50">Field 6</th>
                    <th width="175">Field 7</th>
                </tr>

                <xsl:for-each
select="$Table[Field1=$Field1]">

                <xsl:sort select="Field 3"
order="ascending"/>
                <xsl:sort select="Field 4"
order="ascending"/>
                    <tr>
                        <td>
                            <a>
                                <xsl:attribute
name="href">
                                    <xsl:text>#</xsl:
text>
                                </xsl:attribute>
                                <xsl:attribute
name="onclick">
                                    <xsl:text>window.
open('../New/Details.aspx?Id=</xsl:text>
```

```
                                        <xsl:value-of
select="Field9" />
                                        <xsl:text>',
'new', 'toolbars=no scrollbars=yes')</xsl:text>
                                    </xsl:attribute>
                                    View
                                </a>
                            </td>
                            <td align="center">
                                <xsl:value-of
select="Field 2" />
                            </td>
                            <td>
                                <xsl:value-of
select="Field 3" />
                            </td>
                            <td>
                                <xsl:choose>
                                    <xsl:when test="Field
4!=''">
                                        <xsl:variable
name="Date" select="Field 4" />
                                            <Field 4>
                                                <!--
Month -->
                                                <xsl:valu
e-of select="substring($Date,6,2)"/>
                                                <xsl:text
>/</xsl:text>
                                                <!-- Day
-->
                                                <xsl:valu
e-of select="substring($Date,9,2)"/>
                                                <xsl:text
>/</xsl:text>
                                                <!-- Year
-->
                                                <xsl:valu
e-of select="substring($Date,1,4)"/>
                                            </Field 4>
                                        </xsl:when>
                                    <xsl:otherwise>
                                        <Field 4/>
                                    </xsl:otherwise>
                                </xsl:choose>
                            </td>
                            <td>
                                <xsl:value-of
select="Field 5" />
```

```
                                </td>
                                <td align="center">
                                    <xsl:value-of
select="Field 6" />
                                </td>
                                <td>
                                    <xsl:value-of
select="Field 7" />
                                </td>
                            </tr>
                        </xsl:for-each>
                    </table>
                    <br />
                    <br />
                    </xsl:if>
                </xsl:for-each>
             </xsl:template>
          </xsl:stylesheet>
```

Question 105: XSL:sort

I am trying to sort all entry elements alphabetically by Title and have the output in XML. My document has the following structure:

```
<root>

  <entry>
    <header>
      <index>A1</index>
      <entryTitle>Alligators</entryTitle>
    </header>
    <description>text text text</description>
  </entry>

  <entry>
    ...
  </entry>
</root>
```

I was thinking something along the lines of this, but no such luck.

```
<xsl:stylesheet version="1.0"
   xmlns:xsl="http://www.w3.org/1999/XSL/Transform">
<xsl:output method="xml" />
```

```
<xsl:template match="/">
  <xsl:apply-templates>
    <xsl:sort select="root/entry/header/entryTitle"
/>
  </xsl:apply-templates>
</xsl:template>
```

Is debugging XSL the best way to go about solving this problem?

A: First you need to understand where to place <xsl:sort>.

It is the correct place to put <xsl:sort>. It can be first child of either <xsl:for-each> or <xsl:apply-templates>. It's normally better to use templates where possible, both for readability and extensibility, although it sometimes makes sense to use a for-each (when a nodeset draws from differently named elements for example).

You've got the right kind of idea with your code, but there's a couple of things you should know. When you use <xsl:apply-templates> and you don't specify a template, nodes will match against the default template, which will output the value of the node (ie not the XML). To change the behavior, use a template which matches all nodes and attributes:

```
<xsl:template match="@*|node()">
  <xsl:copy>
    <xsl:apply-templates select="@*|node()"/>
  </xsl:copy>
</xsl:template>
```

This will output the XML of the node. In your case, you need to override the root node behavior to sort the entry elements:

```
<?xml version="1.0" encoding="UTF-8"?>
<xsl:stylesheet version="1.0"
xmlns:xsl="http://www.w3.org/1999/XSL/Transform">
  <xsl:output method="xml" indent="yes"/>
  <xsl:template match="@*|node()">
    <xsl:copy>
      <xsl:apply-templates select="@*|node()"/>
    </xsl:copy>
  </xsl:template>
  <xsl:apply-templates select="root">
```

```
    <root>
      <xsl:apply-templates select="entry">
        <xsl:sort select="header/entryTitle"/>
      </xsl:apply-templates>
    </root>
  </xsl:apply-templates>
</xsl:stylesheet>
```

You final stylesheet should look like this:

```
<?xml version="1.0" encoding="UTF-8"?>
<xsl:stylesheet version="1.0"
xmlns:xsl="http://www.w3.org/1999/XSL/Transform">
  <xsl:output method="xml" indent="yes"/>
  <xsl:template match="@*|node()">
    <xsl:copy>
      <xsl:apply-templates select="@*|node()"/>
    </xsl:copy>
  </xsl:template>
  <xsl:template match="root">
    <root>
      <xsl:apply-templates select="entry">
        <xsl:sort select="header/entryTitle"/>
      </xsl:apply-templates>
    </root>
  </xsl:template>
</xsl:stylesheet>
```

Some rules you might want to remember:

1. xsl:sort applied within apply-templates.

1a. As ma77c noted, it is a typo of JMC. With that amended, I add this note. It is not need to have <root></root> there. In fact, having it there is an anti-climax, making the template defective! No, it should not be there.

1b. In the specific overriding template, for a reasonable requirement is to preserve the attributes as well. Otherwise, you can easily verify for a commonly tag with attribute like:

```
    <root status="expanded">
        <!-- etc etc -->
    </root>
```

You will see that the output would have the status attribute lost. Hence, combining the remarks [1a] and [1b], the XSL would much improve like this:

```
<?xml version="1.0"?>
<xsl:stylesheet version="1.0"
xmlns:xsl="http://www.w3.org/1999/XSL/Transform">
<xsl:output method="xml" encoding="utf-8"
indent="yes" />
<xsl:template match="node()|@*">
    <xsl:copy>
        <xsl:apply-templates select="node()|@*" />
    </xsl:copy>
</xsl:template>
<xsl:template match="root">
    <xsl:copy>
        <!-- [1b] adding this -->
        <xsl:apply-templates select="@*" />
        <xsl:apply-templates select="entry">
            <!-- [1a] taking out spurious "root" -->
            <xsl:sort select="header/entryTitle" />
        </xsl:apply-templates>
    </xsl:copy>
</xsl:template>
</xsl:stylesheet>
```

2. xsl:sort applied within xsl:for-each. As noted, you can actually use sort in two general circumstances, within xsl: apply-templates and within xsl:for-each element. Here, I can show how to realize the same functionality with xsl:sort element so positioned.

```
<?xml version="1.0"?>
<xsl:stylesheet version="1.0"
xmlns:xsl="http://www.w3.org/1999/XSL/Transform">
<xsl:output method="xml" indent="yes" />
<xsl:strip-space elements="*" />
<xsl:template match="node()|@*">
    <xsl:copy>
        <xsl:apply-templates select="node()|@*" />
    </xsl:copy>
</xsl:template>
<xsl:template match="root">
    <xsl:copy>
        <xsl:apply-templates select="@*" />
        <xsl:for-each select="entry">
            <xsl:sort select="header/entryTitle"/>
```

```
            <xsl:apply-templates select="." />
        </xsl:for-each>
    </xsl:copy>
</xsl:template>
</xsl:stylesheet>
```

Index

www.ingramcontent.com/pod-product-compliance
Lightning Source LLC
LaVergne TN
LVHW022318060326
832902LV00020B/3531
* 9 7 8 1 9 3 3 8 0 4 3 9 2 *